Writers of Wales

EDITORS

MEIC STEPHENS   R. BRINLEY JONES

MRS ANNE ADALIZA PUDDICOMBE

(Allen Raine)

1836–1908

Sally Jones

ALLEN
RAINE

University of Wales Press
on behalf of the Welsh Arts Council

1979

Allen Raine is unique in the annals of literature in Wales; not only did she become a best-seller whose sales were counted in millions, but she did so without ever ceasing to write chiefly about one small corner of Cardiganshire. Perhaps the only equivalents, before or since, have been Richard Llewellyn and Leslie Thomas, whose total sales now probably exceed hers; but neither writer entirely matches her own achievement. Despite his many other books, Richard Llewellyn is still first and foremost the author of one, HOW GREEN WAS MY VALLEY; while Leslie Thomas, though he acknowledges his Welsh roots, belongs to the world of Anglo-America rather than Anglo-Wales.

Yet despite her uniqueness and ancient fame, today Allen Raine is forgotten by most of her fellow countrymen or, if remembered, misjudged or misquoted. To some extent her reputation suffers from those very qualities which made her a best-seller; in the century of Dickens it was no drawback to be an absorbing story-teller, and when all novels were suspect as frivolous, romances bore no special brand of iniquity. But when Allen Raine began to write, the dividing line had already been reached, and it is extremely difficult for us now to pass an unbiased judgement on one who wrote in the older tradition, but without that gift of genius which makes JANE EYRE or DAVID COPPERFIELD as acceptable today as when they were first published. Yet there was much more to the novels of Allen Raine than *the simple but romantic love stories* of one critic's description.

There is another reason for the current neglect of Allen Raine in Wales in that, although a handful of critics have worked to establish an ancestry of several centuries for the Anglo-Welsh literary tradition, it is still generally assumed that the movement began with the publication in 1915 of MY PEOPLE, Caradoc Evans's first collection of short stories. Anyone writing before that date is thought to have been either of minor importance or to have been essentially an English writer using the romantic properties of Wild Wales as a picturesque background. As it happens, Allen Raine falls into neither category, as even a cursory glance at her life and work will demonstrate; but since her novels have been out of print for forty years, and the retiring Mrs. Puddicombe of Tresaith who was the 'real Allen Raine' attracted no biographer during her years of fame, the critics have some excuse for their attitude.

Anne Adaliza Evans, who was to become the novelist Allen Raine, was born on 6th October, 1836, in Newcastle Emlyn, Carmarthenshire. Ada (her family name) was the eldest child of

Benjamin Evans, a local solicitor, and his wife Letitia, and she was to be followed by two brothers and a sister; it was not a large family, but it seems to have had the typical Victorian closeness, and though she spent much of the latter part of her life outside Wales, Ada never moved far from the circle of her own kin.

The Evans family came from a social class which, if not precisely obscure, has been very little studied. Nineteenth-century Wales had no true middle class; it had a squirearchy which at its high point merged into the aristocracy, and a peasantry which, lacking natural leaders from the gentry, had produced its own heroes and almost its own culture. Between these two extremes there existed a group—scarcely a class—which was made up of what one might call the 'administrators', those who carried out the orders of the magistrates, who ran the schools, churches and chapels, who practised such medicine as was available, and were generally responsible for the smooth running of society. They were not always a popular group, if only because the measures which they had to carry out often bore harshly on the common man, but because, as professionals, these men and their families had contacts outside their own immediate area, they were also a valuable source of cultural exchange and influence. They were rarely landowners on a large scale; they might own a substantial house in its own grounds, perhaps a farm or two, but little more than that. And just because of this, and because of their necessary contact with the people around them, they were unlikely to idealise either the peasantry from whom they were not far removed or the squirearchy whom they so often served.

Benjamin Evans and his wife were typical of this group. Benjamin's father had been agent to a landed estate, and his maternal grandfather was the Reverend David Davis, Castell Hywel (1745–1827), Unitarian minister, teacher and friend of the philosopher Richard Price and other Radical figures of the late eighteenth century; 'Dafis Castellhywel' was also an author and translator, his best-known work being perhaps his translation of Gray's Elegy into Welsh. Unitarianism, which has always been strong in West Wales, was a branch of Nonconformity particularly attractive to religious intellectuals of an independent turn of mind. Benjamin Evans himself was a faithful member of the Anglican church, but David Davis did not die until Benjamin was eighteen, and the contacts between the Evanses of Newcastle Emlyn and the Davis uncles (who had followed their father into the Unitarian ministry) were maintained in later years.

Letitia Grace, Ada's mother, came from much the same background as her husband. Her father, Thomas Morgan, was a surgeon in Newcastle Emlyn, and her grandfather (or possibly great-grandfather) was Daniel Rowland of Llangeitho, one of the leading figures of the Methodist Revival in Wales. This connection, though illustrious, remains a little vague in the family history, and the Nonconformist link was always with the Unitarian tradition rather than with that of the *Hen Gorff*. Letitia Evans herself is a somewhat shadowy figure. Her portrait shows her as an

4

elderly woman with a gentle face, and though she lived long enough to see her daughter Ada married, she seems to have made little or no lasting impression on her family. The one thing which they did remember about her was of particular interest here, however, since she was apparently an extremely fine story-teller, and in later years her elder daughter attributed her gift of narrative to her mother's early example.

Thus Ada Evans's home was one which, if not especially intellectual, was certainly open to most of the cultural influences of the period. Her father is said to have been something of a scholar, and when his elder daughter began to show signs of unusual ability he took a pride in encouraging her. Ada was a quiet child who gave the impression of being older than her years; she liked roaming about Newcastle Emlyn, especially in the direction of the castle ruins, but she was also fond of the company of the old 'characters' of the town, and of the many stories they had to tell. How far she was actually allowed to wander about by herself in that more rigorous age is not clear, but in any case by the time she was ten, her parents had decided to send her to school in Carmarthen, where she spent three years.

Carmarthen was a regional capital then as now, but it is doubtful whether the girls' schools there would have provided more than the usual polite accomplishments desirable for social and matrimonial success. At any rate, Benjamin Evans seems to have decided that Ada and her sister Lettie needed something more than this, and when Ada was about thirteen years old, he arranged for the two of them to go to Cheltenham, to become part of the household of the Reverend and Mrs. Henry Solly. Mr. Solly was a Unitarian minister and a man of many literary friendships; he knew Dickens, and Mrs. Henry Wood, George Eliot and Bulwer Lytton are all mentioned as visitors either at Cheltenham or at Wandsworth (to which he moved in 1851) so that the girls spent their adolescence in what was apparently a highly intellectual atmosphere. They stayed with the Sollys, at Cheltenham and Wandsworth, for seven years, from 1849 to 1856.

Once Ada's education came to an end, her parents asked Mrs. Solly to arrange that she (and Lettie, presumably) should have some experience of the pleasures and opportunities of life in London. These were somewhat muted, since her diary, beginning in 1856 with a visit to London, describes a round of parties, singing classes and chapel-going, interspersed with less exciting activities such as roaming about the grounds, trimming bonnets and having lessons in leatherwork. There were occasional high spots; on 29th May she records *Peace rejoicings* (for the end of the Crimean War). *Went to Mrs. Case's and saw the fireworks on Primrose Hill. Did not get home till 3 next morning because the streets were so crowded.*

Tom, the brother next to her in age, was a medical student, and there were outings with him to Astley's Theatre and similar displays. Mrs. Solly forbade the girls to visit Tom at University Hall, but they often saw him at Chapel; it is an odd mixture of earnestness and frivolity. One senses a certain 'distance' between Mrs. Solly

6

and her visitors, though they kept in touch for many years; perhaps the portrait of the young Welsh girl suddenly exiled in Manchester or Monmouthshire and half-despised for her country ways and Welsh speech, which appears in three of the novels, is partly autobiographical.

Ada seems to have seen her return home in 1856 as a watershed in her life. She was twenty years old in October and wrote a verse in her diary:

> *To cherished joys of early years*
> *Jesus forgive these parting tears*
>
> ───────────
>
> *Oh yes there is a balm*
> *A kind physician there*
> *My fever'd brain to calm*
> *And wish me not despair*
> *And now dear Saviour set me free*
> *And I will all resign to thee.*

Perhaps she had a foreboding that resignation would soon be called for; on 14th November, a month after Tom had gone back to London for the autumn term, the Evanses learned that he had typhoid fever after eating bad oysters, and on 22nd November he died; he was eighteen years old. On 5th December, in a season of rain and dull weather, Ada recorded simply *Very miserable*. She was not one to pour her heart out, even in a private diary, and the depth of her sorrow, then or later, is best judged from the degree of her silence.

The sixteen years between 1856 and 1872 when she married seem in retrospect to have been largely

a period of stagnation. Mr. Evans had been enlightened enough to give his daughters the best
education available within his means, but he
could not thereafter provide them with any
appropriate outlet for the abilities thus developed.
Lettie, who was extremely pretty, had a fine
singing voice which was trained by Manoel
Garcia, a professor at the Royal Academy of
Music, who was also tutor to Jenny Lind, but
there was no question of a public career for
Lettie; in due course she married Nathaniel
Thomas, Vicar of Llanddarog, and died, childless,
in 1890. Ada had no obvious talent of that sort,
though she too was musical, but eventually she
was to transform Lettie's non-existent career into
the dramatic triumphs of Mifanwy in A WELSH
SINGER. Perhaps in one sense the Evanses were
too much at ease; had they been less comfortable,
then the girls might have been forced to make
use of the skills they had acquired, as were the
Brontë sisters in their bleak nest at Haworth;
poverty and frustration may not be desirable,
but they have often played an important part in
the growth of talent. As it was, Ada and Lettie
settled into a placid routine of calls, paid and
received; visits to relatives; walks and rides
around Newcastle Emlyn; trips to Church with
their father on Sunday mornings and to Chapel
with their mother on Sunday evenings. Yet life
was by no means idle; Ada undertook her share
of the household tasks, and there is one diary
entry, for 17th March, 1860, which is a strange
echo of the famous Brontë birthday papers; it
was her brother Johnny's fifteenth birthday, and
she was very tired because she had been making
cakes and washing her cuffs and collars; she

8

remembered Johnny's birth, and wondered where she herself would be in fifteen years time.

Every summer the family moved from Newcastle Emlyn to the seaside village of Tresaith, some twelve miles away, where Benjamin Evans had taken a fifty year lease on Glandwr, a large house reputedly designed by Nash. Although Newcastle Emlyn could scarcely be described as 'metropolitan', country life at Tresaith was clearly even more to Ada's liking. She was interested in botany and had a deep, though apparently unsentimental, love for animals (including a crotchety parrot which she could handle when no-one else could), but most of all she loved—and loved is not too strong a word—the countryside itself, the moorland and farms and cliffs of the Cardiganshire coast. And Glandwr had the advantage of being within riding distance of Newcastle Emlyn so that the men of the family could combine legal duties and family holidays (a dubious advantage, perhaps, when Mr. Evans's gout brought on an occasional fit of bad temper.)

In all this there is no mention of writing, or of any intellectual activity apart from the study of French and Italian, and such evidence as there is of Ada's literary interests and achievements in these years is not very encouraging. She was intelligent, but not an intellectual, and the books she read, where their titles were recorded, were the normal light reading of a woman with her social background. When she was young her father had bought her a complete set of the Waverley novels which she immediately read straight through; after her return from London, she mentions reading DOMBEY AND SON, but otherwise the books listed are unpromising—THE HEIR, FRANK FAIRLESS, and so forth. (The only book, apart from the BIBLE and the MABINOGION, which is mentioned in her own novels is IVANHOE.)

However Newcastle Emlyn did have a 'literary set' of sorts, and soon after her return from London Ada became a member of this. It seems to have been centred on the Leslie family, Scottish in origin but now settled at Adpar, a suburb of Newcastle Emlyn. Another member was the Reverend John Pryce Jones, vicar of the town and a relative of the Evans family, who was responsible for Ada's first public appearance in print. (She had contributed to HOME SUNSHINE, a short-lived magazine edited by the Leslies and their friends, but this hardly counted as a 'public appearance'.) In 1861 the WESTERN MAIL organised a competition for the best 'Enigma' or riddle in verse; the vicar decided to enter and managed to persuade Ada to do the same, though she protested that she stood no chance if the vicar was trying for the prize. In fact, Ada won, with an entry on the theme 'Plate' (with an odd touch of the macabre she took it as meaning 'coffin plate'). Two points emerge from this; first Ada's modesty about her own gifts, and second, the fact that her associates thought of her even then as one with a particular literary ability. But her success had no sequel, or so one must assume.

And yet it was Ada's connection with the literary amateurs of Newcastle Emlyn which was ultimately to lead to the creation of Allen Raine. In the autumn of 1858, when HOME SUNSHINE was being prepared, Ada had come into contact with Nina Leslie, one of the family at Adpar. At first she was not much impressed by Miss Leslie, but in time they came to be on visiting terms, and Ada apparently gave Nina piano lessons. The Leslies were often visited by their cousins, the Puddicombes, in particular by Helen and Alfred, and Nina, at least, evidently hoped for an even closer connection. An entry in Ada's diary on 4th January, 1860, tells the sad (and somewhat ironic) end of Nina's romance:

Nina came for her music, told me she had broken off her engagement to her cousin, or rather he had broken it off with her. I don't think she has much heart, so I did not pity her much, the gentleman has had no loss. She wanted me to read one of his long letters to her, but I would not. I have been teaching her to play "The 'first love' waltzes" which he sent her. (N.B. This gentleman is now my husband. 1873.)

At this time the cousin seems to have been an unknown quantity, and it is not until much later that Beynon Puddicombe makes a personal appearance in the diary. The Puddicombes were related to the Leslies on their mother's side (Beynon's grandmother, Mary Duff, was Lord Byron's childhood love), but on their father's side they were descended from a Devonshire family, and their father himself was a London solicitor.

Beynon worked as foreign correspondent for Smith Payne's Bank, and he and Ada became engaged, very appropriately, on August Bank Holiday Monday, 1871, while they were on a trip

11

to Box Hill. Ada recorded the event in a surprisingly flat manner: *Engaged to B.P. but when it will be I don't know.* She was thirty-four years old, and one wonders whether there was any particular reason for the comparative lateness of the engagement; was Ada unable to face leaving home for good? In any case, she and Beynon were married at Penbryn Church, Tresaith, on 10th April, 1872.

The Puddicombes settled down at Elgin Villas, Addiscombe, near Croydon, where they lived for the next eight years, but it was a depressing start to married life, since Ada was almost constantly ill, with no specific disease, but rather in a general state of invalidism which confined her to a sofa for most of the time. Possibly the illness was psychological rather than physical, the result of moving from the comparatively free life of Glandwr to the formal, confined life of a banker's wife in late Victorian London. There is a passage in NEITHER STOREHOUSE NOR BARN which may convey something of Ada's feelings at this time; it describes the reactions of Olwen Meyric, orphaned daughter of a Welsh country vicar, who goes to live with her aunt in Manchester:

'Poor things,' she thought. 'how dull their lives must be! Always the same wherever we go—the same talk, the same dresses; and if you look at the clock before you enter their houses, you can always tell what they will be doing: middle day—lunch, and the same things on every table; afternoon— tea, and the same talk everywhere; then in the evening, when we ought to be tired with the fresh air, walking or working, comes dinner and dressing up like a doll.'

12

Quite apart from the effects of homesickness, Ada would not have been by any means the first woman of her century to choose ill-health as an unconscious escape route; Florence Nightingale is only the most illustrious of many. The Puddicombes had no children, and it may have been almost a relief for Ada to be able to shut herself up with her books and study the history and literature of the native country for which she had such an intense love—greater, perhaps, than she had realised before she married. This period of illness apparently lasted for ten years, towards the end of which the Puddicombes moved to Winchmore Hill, on the higher ground north of London, which perhaps suited Ada better; even today it has a surprisingly rural air. However the years from 1880 to 1894 are a blank, and one can only guess that now at last, as her health improved, she began to write, She was in her mid-fifties, but for a novelist this was not entirely a late start; Alexandre Dumas is supposed to have said that if one read sufficiently omnivorously, eventually one would be forced to write oneself, and perhaps this is what happened to Ada.

In 1894 the National Eisteddfod included in its programme a competition for the best serial story, written in Welsh or English, characteristic of Welsh life. The prize was eventually shared between a Welsh story and one in English, called YNYSOER, written by Mrs. Beynon Puddicombe. YNYSOER was not published as a book then, but it was serialised in the NORTH WALES OBSERVER, and also, in a Welsh translation, in Y GENEDL, where it was read by Ernest Rhys, who later on described it as *a crude, extraordinary, long-drawn fairy tale, of a certain charm, but with no very clear relation to anything in everyday life.* It is certainly very much less accomplished than its author's first best-seller A WELSH SINGER, and she herself seems not to have wanted to publish it as a novel, though she did buy back the copyright of the book from the Eisteddfod authorities for three guineas. Eventually it was published as WHERE BILLOWS ROLL, after her death, and brought in at least four hundred pounds in royalties. (About this time Ada seems to have adopted her pen-name, Allen Raine, which came to her in a dream; its source is obscure.)

Ernest Rhys's judgement is perhaps too harsh, but WHERE BILLOWS ROLL *is* apprentice work, especially in the handling of the two interlinked stories which run through it; yet it foreshadows a number of later themes in Allen Raine's novels, and its attitudes are those which recur time and again until almost the last book of all. The scene of the story is the Cardiganshire coast around Tresaith and Llangrannog, and 'Ynysoer' itself is a peninsula which becomes an island at high tide; it is inhabited by a tribe known as the Bullets (from a nickname bestowed on a remote ancestor) who are what might be called the 'unrespectable poor'. The Bullets have gradually been segregated on Ynysoer, and the only members of the mainland community who will have anything to do with them are the twins Iolo and Iola Lloyd. The twins rarely attend either church or chapel, but they try to bring education and moral teaching to the people of the island, helped sometimes by their friend, Nesta Morgan. Nesta falls in love with Hugh Gwythern, the

14

vicar's nephew, but in doing so antagonises her cousin William Owen, whom, by family agreement, she is to marry. Owen pressurises Nesta by threatening the Ynysoer community with eviction; she marries him, he is murdered on his wedding night by his father's old mistress, and Dai Bullet, the twins' foster-brother, is suspected of the murder, tried and condemned. Dai expires (of a broken heart) the night before his execution, the twins soon follow, fading away with some unspecified sickness, and Hugh and Nesta are left to marry and build schools and churches on Ynysoer, which Hugh has bought. It is, to say the least, melodramatic.

The story of Iolo and Iola and Dai is unique in Allen Raine's work. The twins have strange spiritual powers and Iolo is a medium; they are in the habit of holding seance-like meetings for the purpose of helping those of their neighbours who are in trouble. Dai has no such powers, though he is bound to Iola both by love and by a spiritual kinship which includes Iolo; but he is also a kind of scapegoat for his people, and his death is the price that they pay for their return to the ordinary community of Abersethin.

Generally speaking, this theme of atonement, with its Biblical echoes, sits uncomfortably with the straightforward, if melodramatic, love story of Nesta and Hugh, though the two plots become interdependent through William Owen, prime mover in both. Presumably the author realised the incongruity, for she made no later attempts to dramatise sermons. (The spiritualist aspect is not as far-fetched as it might appear; interest in such things was common at the turn of the century—one thinks of Yeats and his wife's automatic writing—and Allen Raine herself had had some experience of seances, perhaps as a result of Lettie's death in 1890.) The religious background of WHERE BILLOWS ROLL is considerably more subtle than the primitive, allegedly Noncomformist hypocrisy and cruelty described by Caradoc Evans writing about the same area twenty years later. The 'natural Christianity' of the twins and their friends is contrasted with the worldliness and callousness of Mr. Gwythern (Allen Raine's only example of a 'bad' vicar) and both again with Harris Beulah, the dying Nonconformist minister who *had a mind and a soul enlightened and refined, and (was) therefore continually meeting with rebuffs and trials, as minister to a congregation of rough, uneducated peasants, who were wedded to their own ideas, when they had any; and to whom the slightest deviation from the old-established modes of thought meant 'something wrong'*. (It should be noted that this was not a 'class' judgement; Allen Raine was equally stringent in her comments on the gentry:

rough, coarse . . . men, whose lives were dominated by circumstances of extreme materialism. It is true they all went to church on Sunday: but further than that no thought of anything above the cares of their farms, or sports, and the gross pleasures of eating and drinking, especially the latter, ever crossed their minds.

YNYSOER was written to some extent from memory, since the Puddicombes had been living near London for almost twenty years, and Ada's invalidism probably limited their opportunities for holidays in Cardiganshire. Hence WHERE

BILLOWS ROLL has a certain air of remoteness, as though its author was looking on, rather than taking part in the story, as she usually seems to do in the later novels. Despite this, her descriptions have a remarkable authenticity, a recording of things actually seen and experienced, as in the account of the board-room at Tygwyn Farm

where all the servants were taking their seats for dinner. Its bare, whitewashed walls were exquisitely clean; a long table, black and shining with age and use, stretched from the door to the open lattice window at the further end, and a long bench each side of the table, upon which the servants were ranging themselves, were the only furniture . . . Wooden bowls and wooden spoons were ranged down each side of the table, and each bowl was soon filled with the smoking 'cawl' in which the fowls and bacon, which were now waiting to be eaten (by the mistress and her guests) on the hall table, had been boiled. With his 'cawl', each one had a slice of the large flat barley loaf, and a hunch of the huge cheese.

This calculated picture of pastoral order and abundance is thrown into even sharper relief by a passage just before it, when the Vicar and his nephew visit the hovel of Modryb Ann, the old hag, crazed by the death of her child, who later murders William Owen:

The earthen floor of the passage was so damp and uneven, and the cottage so dark that for some time they could scarcely see anything; when, however, their eyes were accustomed to the gloom, they became aware of a crouching figure sitting under the large open chimney . . . a bundle of sticks lay in the corner from which an old woman was drawing a fresh supply of fuel . . . from a chain in the chimney hung an iron crock containing some porridge. Hugh had never, even in

Ireland, seen a more poverty-stricken house; the earthen floor was unswept, the small window darkened by the dust of years.

This skill in evoking the material world is not matched, however, by an equal skill in the portrayal of character. Iolo and Iola must be among the most unconvincing sixteen-year-olds in literature, and Nesta is almost too childish. Not surprisingly, she is never called on to face the results of her actions; William Owen dies on the eve of their wedding night, and Nesta falls ill from shock on hearing the news, thus avoiding most of the agony of Dai's trial and death. At last she is able to think of it all simply as the *culminating point of a mistake in her life.* But if Nesta is the heroine, it is Modryb Ann, for all her past sins and her melodramatic cursings, who engages much of the author's sympathy. Early on in the story her cat steals her little bit of butter *and as she ate she struck the empty cupboard door with her stick, muttering oaths and curses as she munched her dry crust. She had borne her poverty and misery through the day, with her usual stolid endurance, but this dry and wretched meal seemed the climax of her woes, and the poor darkened soul melted into tears.* Indeed, the ordinary people of the novel, the servants, the Bullets, the clergymen, the peasants, are far more realised, less stereotyped, than the heroes and heroines; one can compare the description of Dai, on trial for poaching, *And as he walked in with his broad shoulders thrown back, and his head held high as was usual with him, he looked the picture of manly strength and beauty,* with the earlier introduction of John Penlan (the real poacher): *He was dressed in good clothes of homespun cloth, his shoes had been well polished, and his slouched felt hat was worn straight on the top of his head—all signs that it was Sunday and that John had been to chapel.*

As has been suggested above, the tone of WHERE BILLOWS ROLL, sympathetic though it is, seems at a slight remove from the community it describes, as though its author was consciously explaining her setting to an audience who knew nothing of rural Wales. Ironically, her intended audience here was in fact Welsh; later, when she was writing for a much wider public, she made few or no concessions to those ignorant of her background. Yet even here, her commitment to her native land is obvious in the remarks and concerns of the characters, as for instance in Miss Anna Mary Lloyd's dissertation on her ancestry:

The Lloyds of Morfa were the real Welsh gentry, my dear, without a drop of English blood in their veins, not like the Lewises of Gwindale, or the Powells of Pentre, for all they hold their heads so high, they are only half and halfs, my dear, with their grand fashionable ways, and their smattering of Welsh!

Allen Raine would certainly have been no upholder of the 'Welsh Not'; when Nesta tries out her painfully acquired English, she and Hugh can only laugh at the result, while Morgan Schoolin's 'showing off' is the occasion for some rather more boisterous humour, compounded by his lack of control over his pupils. Here, as in the later novels, contempt for the Welsh language, as for things Welsh in general, is associated with a character who, if not precisely villainous, is certainly undesirable.

19

The question of Welsh and English naturally leads to another matter, one which usually generates more heat than light. This is the question of dialect and of clarifying the language situation as it exists in a community which is to some extent bilingual. If one is writing a novel which covers a unitary situation, then there is little or no problem; one can simply equate one language with another; but where one has a situation in which two languages are spoken with some fluency, together with dialects of each which are themselves related to the social background, the accurate portrayal of this linguistic picture is complicated, to say the least. Allen Raine, like every other Anglo-Welsh novelist, was criticised for her handling of peasant speech and her method of conveying the fact that her characters were in varying degrees bilingual, a criticism that took the standard form of denying that the forms she employed were ever used in real life. It is a question that has always been in some degree political, a refusal to come to terms with the fact that there are writers in Wales who have no option but to use the English language— but an English language which has been very heavily influenced by Welsh syntax and usage. In general, however, Allen Raine did succeed in conveying a sense of the linguistic background to the uninvolved reader; the purists objected, but suggested no better method.

If certain attitudes recur in Allen Raine's novels, so also do certain themes and situations which constantly reappear, each time slightly altered and refined, until eventually they find a definitive version or their creator no longer needs to use

20

that particular approach. Although the novel was clearly the medium most suited to her talents (her short stories are mostly sketches from unwritten novels), it took some time before she learnt to let the action flow naturally from the interplay of the characters, and at first she made use of a variety of slightly awkward devices to set the tale in motion. The overbearing behaviour of William Owen in WHERE BILLOWS ROLL is just such a device—he is the wicked squire of Victorian melodrama to the life, and it is all the more surprising, therefore, that he, Modryb Ann and even the much-idealised Nesta come to life as something more than mere cardboard images. Another device, which Allen Raine was to use in various forms in her next five novels as a mainspring for the plot, is that of the sacred promise which must not under any circumstances be broken. Here Hugh promises his dying father that he will not marry until his stepmother has either married again or died; but the effect of the promise is not particularly important, since he is able to tell Nesta about it, and it is a story of mistaken identity when his stepmother, who is very young, is taken to be his wife, that keeps the lovers apart.

In the event, good or bad, YNYSOER remained unpublished except in serial form. However, its author must have received some encouragement from her success, for she immediately set to work on a second novel which was completed by June, 1896, when she began to look for a publisher. In the time-honoured tradition of best-sellers, she had rejection after rejection, six in all, before Hutchinson finally accepted the manuscript (which was originally called MIFANWY), and it appears that she had to contribute something herself towards the cost of publication before Hutchinson would undertake to publish it. The book was retitled A WELSH SINGER, and came out in August 1897; by July 1908 it had sold 316,000 copies.

At this point one first comes into contact with what might be termed the 'breadwinner myth'. According to this, Ada Puddicombe turned to novel-writing and so became Allen Raine in order to support herself and her husband who was incapacitated by illness, and it was her money which paid for Bronmôr, the Puddicombes' holiday home at Tresaith, built in 1897. After her death her brother John publicly denied this story, but it is of some interest because of the possible effects of such a situation on the type of book that Allen Raine was to write. Beynon Puddi-combe did become mentally ill and retired early from his post at Smith Payne's Bank, and in 1900 the Puddicombes moved to Bronmôr as their permanent home.

Most accounts suggest that Beynon's illness began in 1900, but it seems more probable that it was a slow decline into whatever form of breakdown or disease he suffered from, and that the building of Bronmôr was partly influenced by the likeli-hood of a need for a place of retirement near family or friends who could help in case of emergency. Beynon Puddicombe had held a post of responsibility, and the Bank allowed him an extremely generous pension of £25 a month, quite apart from any other income or savings which he might have acquired, so that clearly there was no need for his wife to support him. On the other hand, medical care could be expensive, and Puddicombe had to spend periods away from home, in a private asylum in North Wales, which eventually cost £4 a week; he also had an attendant with him constantly, a man called Ferrier. (The precise nature of the illness is not known, but it probably involved periods of violence, and his behaviour was completely unpredictable from day to day.) Obviously any extra money would be useful. It is possible, too, that Ada had another reason for welcoming the opportunity to make some money of her own; she had had to ask her husband for the £20 which Hutchinson wanted as a contribution to the cost of A WELSH SINGER, and it had been given none too graciously. Her young nephew Roy, John's son, who was staying with them at the time, remembered Puddicombe saying *Well, we must humour the little woman.*

Whatever the financial stimulus may have been, A WELSH SINGER was set firmly in the mould of the popular novel of Late Victorian literature, and in this it is to some extent untypical of Allen Raine's novels. It begins, like the rest, in the coastal region of South Cardiganshire and tells the story of two orphans, Ieuan and Mifanwy, who work for John Powys, a local farmer, whose niece Elizabeth loves Ieuan and hates Mifanwy. Ieuan, a promising sculptor, is adopted by Sir Glynne Meredith, the local boy made good; but before going to London to be trained, he promises to return and marry Mifanwy. Elizabeth Powys also goes to London to have her voice trained professionally. (Ieuan, incidentally, discovers that he is really the son of John Powys and Sir Glynne's sister.) Mifanwy, left at home in Abersethin, grows too old to be a shepherdess and, on her way to Merthyr to look for work, falls in with a circus and, in her turn, goes to London where her singing voice is discovered. Rhys Morgan, once vicar of Abersethin and now a London clergyman, arranges for her education, and she becomes an overnight success. Ieuan, now a 'gentleman' and regretting his promise to marry Mifanwy, falls in love with the new singer, La Belle Russe (i.e. Mifanwy) but at last, after a fire (fanned by the jealous Elizabeth), recognises his childhood love.

The story is preposterous, but no more so than the average romance of that period—no more so, indeed, than the plot of JANE EYRE. Singers and actresses were popular heroines, while the Cinderella story which lies behind the novel is the hardiest perennial of all fairy-tales. Even Mifanwy's shepherdess role is typical of an age that delighted in paintings of well-fed peasant children in decorative rags. All these features belong to the standard English tradition of popular literature at the turn of the century, and since they are allied to an easy and gripping narrative style, one can only be surprised, not by the success of the novel, but by the reluctance of publishers to accept it in the first place. It seems likely that the book fell foul of one of the prejudices of the London publishing world in that it had a Welsh setting and characters— something that never seems to deter the reading public in general, but for some reason arouses antipathy among metropolitan publishers and critics. Once A WELSH SINGER had succeeded, of course, there was no objection to its author's writing about Wales as often as she liked, but the novelist Owen Rhoscomyl, writing to her family after her death, speaks particularly of his admiration for her work in *breaking down the antipathy to stories dealing with Wales.*

Although in terms of construction and technique, A WELSH SINGER is a considerable advance on YNYSOER, it is in many ways a far less sophisticated piece of work. Allen Raine knew London, from her adolescence at least, and no doubt 'Pomfrey's grand circus' had its origins in her visits to Astley's Amphitheatre with Tom, just as Mifanwy's career grew out of Lettie's music lessons. The Welsh scenes, however, have an authenticity that makes them very different from the 'picturesque' descriptions of people and places of the English novelist-cum-tourist. Any Anglo-Welsh writer who takes Wales for a theme is bound to find him or herself acting to some extent as an instructor, since the loss of (or ancestral ignorance of) the Welsh language means also the loss of a knowledge of things Welsh in the broader sense. This applies both ways—the Welsh-speaker is as likely to be ignorant of the social customs of the mining valleys of Southeast Wales as the non-Welsh-speaker is of the habits of rural Cardiganshire—and to be Anglo-Welsh in the literary sense is also to be a bridge between three communities, Welsh, Anglo-Welsh and English. It is extremely unlikely that Allen Raine, writing in the 1890s, was consciously aware of this, but in practice this is precisely what she achieves.

A WELSH SINGER contains very few footnotes for
the benefit of its non-Welsh audience (TORN SAILS,
the next novel, perhaps as a result, breaks out in
a rash of them), but the quirks of social behaviour are observed with a precision that is both
understanding and detached, as in the description
of John Powys's 'lying in state':

*She escorted each fresh visitor through the long passage and
into the darkened room, turning down the sheet that covered
the dead man's face, and reverently replacing it when the
visitors had gazed solemnly for a few minutes; then, accompanying them back to the room in which Mrs. Powys was
seated, she placed a chair for them in a row with the other
callers, who were ranged round the walls. Each woman
sniffed a little, and wiped a tear away with the corner of
her best apron, the bettermost farmers' wives unfolding a
clean pocket handkerchief for the occasion, and keeping it
clasped between their two hands for the rest of the visit,
never returning it to their pockets until they were well on
their way home, and out of sight of the house. Everyone
brought with her or him some substantial proof of sympathy,
in the shape of provisions, which were silently placed on the
table in front of Mrs. Powys, who returned thanks with as
much show of gratitude as if she had been really in need
of them.*

It is almost with a sense of shock that one moves
from this to a passage like that which describes
Ieuan's sensations when he hears La Belle Russe
singing:

*it was inexplicable to him, this tumult of feeling that her
voice raised in him. The wash of the sea seemed to be really
in his ears; a vision of the cliffs, and the sheep, and the
rugged paths, where a boy and a girl stood close together,*

rose up before him. Yes! and the very sound of his own long forgotten words, 'I will return to thee, lass! Hast ever known me break a promise?'

It is this promise, a contrivance for the benefit of the plot, which leads to many of the weaknesses and absurdities of the novel—Ieuan's failure to recognise Mifanwy in London being perhaps the most outstanding. The main characters also suffer from over-romanticisation. Mifanwy herself is unbelievably sweet and innocent for one brought up as a parish orphan and constantly subject to the malice of the Powys family. Ieuan is less angelic; he means well, but is easily corrupted by his new social status so that though he cannot bring himself to disown Mifanwy and his foster parents, he speaks of them as creatures less capable of fine feelings and actions, as when he tells La Belle Russe about his childhood sweetheart:

'Oh, she felt (our parting) very much, as I did, at the time; but she soon got over it, I suspect. Shortly afterwards, she also left her home, and went into service somewhere or other, and is now, I suppose, a smart little maid with white cap and apron. And so ends my romance.'

Indeed, in some ways A WELSH SINGER is a study of snobbery. Ieuan, though orphaned, has two families—the Powyses and the Merediths—both of whom are socially respectable; he also has talent. And yet Mifanwy, the child of a small farmer and his wife, with no advantages save her native ability and her innocence and good nature, outstrips Ieuan and in effect redeems him from his folly.

Some idea of the distance between YNYSOER and A WELSH SINGER can be drawn from a comparison of the two 'villains', William Owen and Elizabeth Powys. William Owen is a stage villain, but Elizabeth Powys is a very different creature, the first of a succession of 'duplicate heroines', women who are closely linked with the heroine herself, in an association of love, hate or both, and whose actions, often violent, precipitate a climax or climaxes in the story in a way that is often more positive than the heroine's own activities. Elizabeth is beautiful and talented, but she lacks any real depth of feeling, and as she has no capacity for loving, so she has no real capacity for suffering; on waking from a faint brought on by the realisation of what she has done by locking Mifanwy in her dressing room while the fire rages, *'Mrs. Elliott, where is my jewel box?' were her first words; and it was only the sight of the box, which Mr. Camperton held up to her, that soothed her into quietness.*

And yet A WELSH SINGER, for all its fairy-tale elements, is no Gothic romance; Elizabeth Powys convinces where a more lurid villainess would have ruined the effect.

A WELSH SINGER seems to have been immediately successful, and over the next ten years Allen Raine turned out eight novels, almost one a year. In her second published novel she reverted to a wholly Welsh setting and kept to this thereafter. This, TORN SAILS, is possibly Allen Raine's best-known book; it is certainly the one most often associated with her name, and it is no doubt responsible for the impression that her books were mainly 'everyday stories of fisherfolk'.

28

Unfortunately it is by no means her best work, being in parts almost as contrived and melo-dramatic as the worst specimens of 'Anglo-Welshery', while its heroine is so passive that she arouses irritation rather than admiration in the reader.

The story is the first of what might be called variations on a quartet, and it is set in Tresaith, this time under the name of Mwntseison. Hugh Morgan owns the sailmaking business on which the village depends; he is a villager rather than a 'gentleman' but his benevolence and his sail works have made him both the most important and the best-loved figure in Mwntseison. He is unmarried (though on friendly terms with Mari Vone, the sweetheart whom he rejected after a tiff many years before), and looks on Ivor Parry, his second-in-command, as his heir. Ivor is in love with Gwladys Price, one of the sail-makers, and she with him, but they have come to no spoken understanding, and while Ivor is away on business, Hugh, who has become infatuated with Gwladys, proposes to her and is accepted. Ivor returns and discovers that Gwladys loves him, but they decide that the wedding must go on; for Gwladys to break her promise would be to shame Hugh before the whole community. Ivor goes away, and only Gwen, his former sweetheart, knows the truth. Hugh and Gwladys's marriage is unsatisfactory, and Ivor's return to the village does not help; meanwhile Gwen, respectably married but maddened now by the death of her baby, drops malicious hints to Hugh, who realises that his infatuation is dead, but is still angered by the rumours. Although events demonstrate

the absolute purity of Ivor and Gwladys, it is
only Gwen's madness which resolves the problem, when she burns down the sailmaking shed,
thus causing both her own death and that of
Hugh. Two years later Mari Vone also dies and
is buried with Hugh, while Ivor and Gwladys
presumably live happily ever after.

This is clearly a different sort of novel to A WELSH
SINGER where the characters involved do not
change in relation to one another; one knows
that Ieuan will not turn to Elizabeth or Mifanwy
marry Tom Pomfrey, whatever the provocation.
On the other hand, Allen Raine wrote always in
one particular form, that of the romance, and
one basic tenet of this is that the ending must
be 'happy'. All manner of horrors may come
between, but in the end the lovers must be sorted
out and given the right partners, even if they
have to die to be united. It has always been
critically fashionable to decry this literary form
as not worth serious consideration; and certainly
much of it is as clearly a commercial product as
a washing machine. This, then, is a chief reason
for the past critical neglect of Allen Raine; not
only was the form that she chose regarded as in
some way 'beneath' the average critic, but also
the critics themselves were unlikely to come
across her work in the normal course of events.
(Emlyn Williams, who was greatly influenced by
A WELSH SINGER, came across it as a small boy,
in the box of his mother's maidservant). We do
not know whether Allen Raine chose to write
romances because they were financially more
rewarding, or whether she herself preferred pure
story-telling; but the result of her choice was to

produce books which have almost a dual nature. On the one hand there is the sober, precise, even witty depiction of the rural society of which she was herself a part, and on the other hand there are passages of what can only be described as romantic gush, and a variety of awkward, creaking devices intended to bring about the appropriate happy ending which, if they do not always falsify the internal logic of the story, certainly sit very oddly alongside the social observation of the background.

TORN SAILS is a particularly obvious example of the bad effects of this deliberate contriving. Once again Allen Raine uses the theme of the unbreakable promise to set events in motion, though here more than in any other of her novels there is little justification for it. When the promise is made, the reasons for not breaking it are more or less valid, given Hugh's place in the community; the banns have been called and the matter made public, so that for Gwladys to withdraw would be far more serious than a mere jilting (of the kind that Hugh himself had practised on Mari Vone). Thus the keeping of the promise is given almost an ethical content. Yet after the mistake has been made, instead of seeking a rapid resolution of the problem, the author goes on to show that nobility is not enough. The marriage that results is barren in every way, and yet cannot be escaped except through the tragedy of Hugh's death. One contrivance leads to another, and the promise leads inevitably to the fire and to the equally novelettish device of Mari Vone's mysterious but

31

painless decline so that she can finally be united with her lost love. It is a confusing mixture of ethics and story-telling.

Behind this creaky main plot, however, lies the story of Gwen and her family, the source of much of the best writing in the book. Gwladys, even for a heroine, is a passive character, one who rarely, if ever, does more than react to the behaviour of others. Gwen is a very different matter. At first her malice is simply that of the rejected sweetheart who is jealous and so aware of every action that passes, but she comes of strange stock:

'My little one—born in lawful wedlock, too! Not like thee, mother, nor granny, not yet her mother!'

'No, indeed, it is true!' said Lallo, rocking herself backwards and forwards; 'bad luck has followed us for generations. But thy father was a respectable man, Gwen; he is deacon in his chapel at Abersethin, and his wife and family are the best dressed in Salem Chapel.'

Gwen's grandmother, Peggi Shân, was famous locally as a witch, and when Gwen's child dies, partly from the effects of her weird remedies, *'it pleases her to think she has the same "hysbys" nature'*, and the combination of grief and ancestral influences sends her mad. This, if at times melodramatic, is a logical part of the story, but it leads to a number of passages discussing madness in rural communities which read somewhat oddly when one considers the author's own problems in that connection. Indeed, the fact that she could speak of these matters at all suggests a writer very different from the romantic idealist of most

32

critical accounts; there is nothing picturesque in Gwen's insanity. The romantic idealist did exist, of course; one has only to look at the passage describing Mari Vone's peaceful end:

He knew that that gentle spirit had quitted the beautiful tenement in which it had lived for thirty-seven years . . . he sat beside her while the sun sank below the horizon; the grassy pillow on which she lay shone with the burnished gold of its last rays, which threw also with its last kiss a rosy flush over Mari's face.

Yet this stands side by side with passages like the following:

Where intermarriage is so common . . . peculiarities of character gather strength with every succeeding generation . . . insanity is always lurking amongst the seeming calmness and rural simplicity of the village life, ever ready to pounce upon the harassed in mind or body. It is no uncommon thing to see in a small village containing two or three hundred inhabitants, two or three windows boarded and barred, behind which are kept the unhappy sufferers from this terrible fate. The dread of the asylum hangs like a cloud over the scene that appears such a picture of rustic happiness.

If one allows for the stylistic differences, this is Caradoc Evans country; there is one episode when Gwen unintentionally chokes the baby while feeding it a mixture of roasted mouse, brown sugar and butter, which cannot help but remind one of old Nanny and her rats in BE THIS HER MEMORIAL.

TORN SAILS was once again an immense success;

indeed it seems to have been the most popular of Allen Raine's books in Wales, and it was made into a film in the early nineteen twenties. (The filming took place at Llangrannog and New Quay, and local interest was enough to draw audiences into Llandysul from as far away as Pencader, even though it meant a six-mile walk home afterwards.) The books that followed, By BERWEN BANKS and GARTHOWEN, followed the model of TORN SAILS rather than that of A WELSH SINGER, though the melodramatic element grew slowly less.

By BERWEN BANKS at least might well be described as a quiet love story; there is less of the 'social' element in this novel than in any other of Allen Raine's books. It is the story of Valmai, niece of Essec Powell, a grim, penny-pinching Methodist minister, and Cardo Wynne, son of Meurig Wynne, vicar of Abersethin, who meet and fall in love despite family opposition on both sides. The lovers, helped by Cardo's curate friend Gwynne Ellis, are secretly married, but then Cardo is sent to negotiate a reconciliation between his father and his uncle who lives in Australia. He loses his memory in an accident, and while he is thus delayed Valmai's uncle casts her out because she is pregnant. She retreats to Ynysoer, the child is born and dies, and Valmai goes to Monmouthshire to stay with her long-lost sister Gwladys. In due course Cardo recovers, and after further complications caused by Gwladys's misogyny, the lovers are reunited, Gwynne Ellis marries Gwladys, and Essec and Meurig Wynne become friends.

Despite the presence of so many clergymen, there is no strong religious element in the novel. Indeed, considering the standard view of nineteenth-century Wales as a country overshadowed by theology in all its forms, Allen Raine's tolerance is surprising. Partly, no doubt, it came from her own upbringing, half church, half chapel, though she was well aware of the religious life that went on around her, and there is a carefully observed account of the 'Sassiwn', an open-air event, and all the preparations leading up to it. However, the 'Sassiwn' itself is chiefly the occasion of a meeting between Cardo and Valmai, and one suspects that the sympathy of the author herself is rather to be found in the unintentional irony of Betto the Maid's comment:

'And the impidence of Essec Powell! What do you think, Caradoc? he is praying for your father—out loud, mind you— in the prayer-meeting every Wednesday evening! But there! the master is beforehand with him, for he is praying for Essec Powell on Tuesdays!'

But if the religious element is not a serious factor, ethical considerations certainly are. Valmai's promise to Cardo not to reveal their marriage, though made in good faith and for sufficient reason, is kept even when to do so brings great suffering; Meurig Wynne's unfounded jealousy of his wife and brother almost loses him his son, and causes him long years of remorse and misery; Gwladys, too, very nearly causes serious harm by her efforts to 'help' Valmai and send Cardo away again. In each case the original ground is in one way or another a mistaken idea of the truth; carried to excess, each

almost causes tragedy, and only the fact that
Allen Raine was writing a romance allows the
dénouement to be happy.

As will be apparent, many of the themes and
situations of the earlier novels recur here. The
key role played by a promise or vow is the most
obvious example, but once again there is the
quartet — Cardo, Valmai, Gwynne Ellis and
Gwladys—though this time there is no question
of their changing partners. There is, too, the
ambiguity of the relationship between Valmai
and Gwladys; Gwladys is the long-lost sister, the
newly-found friend, but she is also very nearly
the cause of a permanent separation between
Valmai and Cardo, an echo of the roles played
by Elizabeth Powys and Gwen. This mixture of
friend and rival persists, though as time goes on,
the rivalry becomes less damaging, and in later
novels the rival herself becomes an object of pity.
(One wonders if Nina Leslie, Beynon's fiancée
and Ada's friend, sat for at least part of this
portrait.)

One theme, however, clearly does come from the
author's own experience, and that is the dis-
cussion of the Welsh language and all things
Welsh, and the attitude to them of the Welsh
people. Allen Raine had no respect for the
*would-be genteel (who) perfectly unconscious of the beauty
of their own language, and ignorant of its literature, affect
English manners and customs, and often pretend that English
is more familiar to them than Welsh, a fatuous course of
conduct which brings upon them only the sarcasm of the
lower classes, and the contempt of the more educated.* Later
in BY BERWEN BANKS she illustrates this in the

36

words of Mrs. Power, Gwladys's adopted mother, who tells Valmai that: ' "*Whatever*" *and* "*indeed*" *so often is very Welshy, my love*' . . . *with a sniff of dis-approval* . . . '*I hope Gwladys won't catch your accent.*' Much more to Allen Raine's liking was Gwynne Ellis's remark, partly ironic in its context, but none the less sincere: '*To know two languages means to look at everything from two points of view* . . . *A man who knows two languages knows half as much again of everything as a man who can only speak one.*' Similar comments appear in novel after novel, at a time when the accepted attitude (except for such mavericks as O. M. Edwards) seems to have been that the true destiny of Wales was to become ever more completely Anglicised, and to merge itself into an ever more glorious 'Great Britain' as defined by London. Thirty years earlier R. D. Blackmore had spoken up for Wales in THE MAID OF SKER, but the critical winds of literary England soon caused him to withdraw into the peaceful countryside of regionalism east of Offa's Dyke, from which he never stirred again. It was a failure of nerve that never affected Allen Raine.

If BY BERWEN BANKS is basically a love story with social embellishments, then GARTHOWEN is its mirror image, since here it is the social setting which is important, and the love story plays the secondary role. There *is* a love story, of course, but it is comparatively muted and involves very little tension or drama; even the 'promise' theme, which recurs for almost the last time, plays no serious part. The full title of the book is GARTHOWEN: A STORY OF A WELSH HOMESTEAD, and this in itself suggests that Allen Raine had something more in mind than a simple romance.

In fact what she produces is a study of the effects of a particular society and its demands and expectations on human beings.

Ebben Owens of Garthowen has two sons, Gethin and Will, and a daughter Ann. Gethin, a sailor, is the black sheep of the family; Ann is engaged to a local minister, Gwilym Morris, who lodges at Garthowen; and Will, the intellectual of the family, wants to become an Anglican clergyman. Ebben, though wealthy in land, has no ready money available for Will's college fees, having lent his cash to neighbours, and to preserve his favourite child from humiliation, steals the forty pounds that Ann and Gwilym have saved for their wedding. Gethin, who has come home, takes his father's guilt on himself and goes away, leaving behind him Morva, the heroine, who loves him, but is promised to Will. (She is the Garthowen maidservant). Will, who is flourishing socially, is too vain to release Morva from her promise, but he himself courts and marries Gwenda Vaughan, niece of a local squire; his 'adoption' by his uncle, Dr. Owen (Ebben's brother, also a clergyman—he has dropped the 's') makes this possible. Though the money is returned, Ebben's conscience torments him until he confesses his crime in a meeting of the 'Sciet' (sic). His fellow deacons, even Jos Hughes whose request for money led to the trouble, reject him, all except Thomas Morgan:

But no-one took any notice of his remark, for he was never considered to have been endowed with his full complement of sense, though his pure and unblemished life had caused him to be chosen deacon.

However Ebben's family stand by him and he is too contrite to notice Will's callous description of his spiritual agonies as a fuss about nothing. Meanwhile Gethin and Morva are united.

In certain ways GARTHOWEN is almost a fore-shadowing of Tegla Davies's GŴR PEN Y BRYN, and to some extent the comparison favours GARTHOWEN, which covers a much wider canvas. (As a minister, Tegla Davies had a professional concern with the theological aspects of remorse and confession.) Ebben Owens is a character of considerable interest, not so much for his spiritual torments (which Allen Raine omits as something private to the man himself), as for the sense in which he is a product of his society. The Owenses are former gentry and so have not only a place to uphold, but certain duties to fulfil, and Ebben, being a proud man, is determined to carry out these duties even if, as happens, it leaves him in personal difficulties. In the novel the problem arises because cash income was a scarce com-modity in West Wales at the turn of the century; Ebben, as Owens of Garthowen, is assumed to have ample funds, though in fact he is neither better nor worse off than his fellows, and has to lend money he cannot readily spare. But in Ebben this pride, which was, in its time and place a necessary social cement, has turned to some-thing very like vanity. He himself is a staunch Nonconformist, but he sees no contradiction in the idea that Will, his much-loved son, shall become an Anglican clergyman. Ebben's brother has already done so, and in the process disowned his own family; it is, so the farmer thinks, a sign of gentility, and not a doctrinal matter at all.

He does not, of course, foresee that Will, too, will consider disowning the family at Garthowen, and when the boy, newly ordained, comes to officiate at Castell On, the nearby town, he shows a pathetic pride in his son. After the service is over, he says, '*We'll wait with the car, at the top of the lane. We won't push ourselves on to him at the church door when all the gentry are speaking to him.*' But Will drives past with his uncle and does not see them, and it is left to Ann and Gwilym to comfort the old man. The disappointment and the chance appropriateness of the text of Will's sermon—'*Lord, try me and see if there be any wicked way in me*'—do much to bring Ebben to the point of confession at the Seiat. Will himself is very much his father's son, but in his case vanity is joined with weakness and a shallowness of feeling that could bode ill for his future.

The main setting of GARTHOWEN, like the other novels, is the south Cardiganshire coast, but this is probably the least maritime of all Allen Raine's books. (In view of the frequent critical references to her books as '*stories of primitive fisherfolk*', it should be pointed out that in fact the communities she describes are basically agricultural and land-based; they exist near the sea-shore, but their inhabitants are farmers, not fishermen). It is not, however, a landlocked setting; Gethin is a sailor and the novel begins in a South Wales port, and returns there later when Sara, Morva's foster-mother, goes to find Gethin and bring him home for the final reunion. Nor is it a deprived area. Allen Raine draws few pictures of serious poverty —her terrors are of the mind rather than of the flesh—but here at least she makes clear the

40

element of communal self-help that often pre-
vented the worst effects of hunger and cold.

*Under Ann's skilful management, in spite of their dwindled
means, Garthowen was always a home of plenty. The
produce of the farm was exchanged at the village shops for
the simple necessaries of domestic life. The sheep on their
own pasture lands yielded wool in abundance for their homespun clothing, the flitches of bacon that garnished the rafters
provided ample flavouring for the cawl—Indeed, there was
only one thing that was not abundant at Garthowen, and
that was—ready money!*

GARTHOWEN shows signs of a development away
from the earlier romances and towards something that might be described as a social novel,
but it was a development that does not seem
to have been entirely popular with the public.
The novel sold well over 200,000 copies, but this
was still less than the 'romances' and the author
seems to have decided (perhaps with some encouragement from her publisher) that it would
be better to forget the social element and concen-
trate on the romantic complications. At any
rate, A WELSH WITCH, the next to be published,
is both a romance and her most ambitious work.
It includes the final re-working of the 'promise'
plot, another variation on the quartet of lovers,
a family feud, shipwrecks, mine disasters, gipsies
and even a sort of Celtic pantheism. The title
itself, with its echo of the title of her first and
most successful published novel, suggests a
return to the earlier style. And yet she managed
to include all this while remaining within
the Welsh context; the events of the novel are
melodramatic, certainly, but they are all possible,

even if the comparatively prosaic reality has been
heightened for dramatic effect. There are no
circuses, no peasant primadonnas this time, but
the public evidently liked the mixture, for the
sales figures soared once again.

A WELSH WITCH tells the story of four young
people: Goronwy Hughes of Sarnissa Farm;
Catrin, daughter of Simon Rees who owns
Pengraig, the neighbouring farm; Yshbel Lloyd
who, left in Treswnd as a baby, has expectations
of future grandeur when her father will return
for her; and Walto Gwyn, only son of the local
'squiress'. Goronwy is a leader among his peers,
but Catrin is an outcast, suspected of witchcraft,
though her wildness is only the product of
neglect and the loss of her mother; Goronwy
gets involved when he makes a rash promise to
rid Treswnd of the supposed witch, but actually
helps to domesticate her, a process completed
when she has to nurse her crippled father (whom
she loves devotedly, despite his past cruelty to
her). Then Goronwy, growing out of childhood,
feels he should start courting, and, not realising
that his friendship with Catrin has become love,
turns to Yshbel—who is drawn to Walto, but
forbidden by Mrs. Gwyn to encourage him on
pain of eviction from her home. The scene is
thus set for a complicated misunderstanding.
Catrin loves Goronwy, and knows it; Goronwy
loves Catrin, but does not realise this, and asks
Yshbel to marry him; Yshbel consents, but loves
Walto and so keeps putting off the wedding;
and Walto, not knowing what his mother has
done, loves Yshbel, but thinks that she rejects

42

him, and so goes off to the 'Works' (Glamorgan) to act as manager of a colliery owned by relatives.

At this point Yshbel's uncle appears and takes her off to Pontargele in Glamorgan where he too owns a colliery (near that where Walto works, naturally). He and his wife are ready to adopt Yshbel, but the latter, for all her childhood dreams of social grandeur, is basically sensible, and soon sees through her uncle's pretensions. Goronwy, having had enough of waiting, also comes to Pontargele, gets work in the mines and arranges to marry Yshbel at once. (Her relatives, shocked that she is connected even by friendship with a mere collier, cast her out, but Walto's kin befriend her.) Fortunately, since the three lovers are all determined to be bound by past promises and friendships, even if it means a lifetime of misery, the local curate sees their folly and forbids the banns. Walto and Yshbel are united at last, though only after Walto and Goronwy survive being trapped in the mine. All three go home to Treswnd, where Catrin has nursed her dying father and then, at his death, left home, unable to bear the thought of seeing Goronwy and Yshbel married. Goronwy follows her to North Wales, and they too are married.

It is plain that this time the emphasis is on the emotional entanglements of the characters, and that the social background, detailed though it is, is a setting for the four lovers, rather than the mainspring of the plot. This is not to say that either Treswnd or Pontargele, or their various inhabitants, are only animated wallpaper; as always with Allen Raine, the social setting has a depth and importance beyond that of mere background material. But on the other hand, the emotional entanglements mentioned above are not only those of straightforward romance. There is, for instance, a close relationship between Catrin and Yshbel, a development of the love-hate rivalry mentioned earlier, and there are the family linkings—Catrin's love for her father, Goronwy's for his grandmother, Yshbel's for her new-found aunt and uncle, Mrs. Gwyn's fierce love for her son. All these give a richness to the book. It should be added that although the adventures of the romantic quartet are one main theme of the book, another is their own individual growth, both mental and spiritual; they begin as pre-adolescents and end as mature men and women.

It has already been suggested that although A WELSH WITCH is particularly full of incident and colour, the elements which provide these are not foreign to Welsh life at that period. Even Catrin's adventures with the gipsies, to whom she is related through her mother, though no doubt calculated to win the favour of an audience familiar with AYLWIN and LAVENGRO, echo many a genuine family anecdote or tradition. 'Teulu Abram Wood', the Welsh gipsies, had their own importance in rural Wales, and old Nancy Wood, the matriarch of the group, is a remarkable character, proud of her clan and of Catrin as a member of it, concerned for Catrin's safety and yet, in a curiously legalistic manner, quite ready to take advantage of the girl's innocence and steal part of her small stock of money.

44

Rather less likely than such dramatic events as Catrin's flight, Captain Hughes's shipwreck, or even the abortive attempt to send Catrin to the Asylum as a lunatic, is the lengthy episode at 'the Works'—less likely, that is, in terms of Allen Raine's predominantly rural interests; the world of the mining valleys was in its own way as much a part of the experience of the people of South Cardiganshire as the coast-wise shipping trade. Here again, one has the sense of something known, and the same grasp of the economic and social setting, as with the collier who compares life at home with the advantages of Glamorgan:

'I'm a Cardi myself, though it's many years since I saw the dear old country. 'Tis true you get a good appetite there, but twelve shillings a week will not give you much to satisfy it. Here we get fresh meat for our dinner, bacon for our breakfast, tishens and pies in plenty, and that's what I call the best things in life—in this life, mind you—for I'm not one who neglects his soul.'

Interestingly, too, one theme of this novel which is almost completely absent elsewhere in the author's work, is social inequality and, to some extent, the class structure. It is a subject appropriate to the industrial novels of the nineteenth century, and it is curious that the theme should appear all of a sudden when Allen Raine turns her attention to this new area. It even affects life in Treswnd, where one has Yshbel's musing on her expectations of better things, and Mrs. Gwyn playing the villainess in order to prevent her son's misalliance.

This 'class' element does not concern itself with
social strife; instead the conflict manifests itself
in the relationship between Yshbel, Goronwy
and Walto, all equal at home, but in Pontargele
living in almost separate worlds, Yshbel with her
nouveau riche relatives, Goronwy with the
colliers, and Walto with his own family who,
though coal owners, come from the ancient
Welsh squirearchy. Yshbel's family are not in
themselves unpleasant; but their good points
are hidden by their foolish attempt at social
grandeur—all the more foolish because the valley
where they live is also the place of their birth,
and everyone knows exactly how they began.
This snobbery has warped their judgement, as
Allen Raine makes clear:

*(Mrs. Jones) walked nervously up and down the room, which
was furnished with every luxury that money and bad taste
could collect. Her black eyes and her mouth had lost their
natural kindly expression in their continual endeavour to
look dignified and indifferent to her grand surroundings.*

Once again the author links characters who are
less than desirable with the rejection of the
Welsh language; one of Mr. Jones's first orders
to his newly-found niece is to *drop the Welsh* and
speak only English.

The real climax of the novel is the explosion in
the mine, when Goronwy, Walto and two other
colliers, one a boy of twelve, are trapped under-
ground for several days, and menaced by rats,
fire-damp, flooding and eventually starvation.
The boy dies and the other collier breaks down

46

into partial insanity. Despite this, the writing never quite tips over into melodrama or senti-mentality; as for cliché, though now all these elements, as well as Yshbel's wait at the pithead, are conventional, in 1902, when the book ap-peared, they were quite new, in fiction at least, and possibly even the first working of the subject. (Almost certainly Allen Raine drew her back-ground material from accounts of the 1890 Morfa Pit disaster and that at Tynewydd in 1877.)

Unfortunately, Allen Raine had taken only three of her four main characters to Pontargele, and Catrin too had, by the logic of the story, to embark on some exploit which would complete her 'growing-up'. Allen Raine chose to send her off with the gipsies, and though this section of the book has its own interest, it is too little integrated with the earlier settings and themes to be successful. Indeed, Catrin's story is always to some extent separate, so that the book tends to become two novels in parallel rather than a single artistic whole. Goronwy, Yshbel and Walto mature, but in the social sense, whereas Catrin's growth is mainly spiritual. Her wild childhood, as described at the beginning of the novel, is the result of neglect, but it has led to the develop-ment in her of a kind of Christian pantheism, and when the vicar cannot answer her request for information on Heaven and Hell, she prays for him (greatly to his discomposure):

'Dear God! I ask You to bless this poor man, and to teach him as You teach me. He doesn't know much, and he wants to feel You near him in the close house and the dark church. Near as You are here on the hillside.'

(The vicar's response is to try to send her to the Asylum to be properly cared for.) Catrin does eventually go to church, but it is the beginning of her domestication, rather than a moment of conversion. This has already happened when, distressed by Goronwy's courtship of Yshbel, she prays that God will destroy her rival, but almost at once repents; when her prayer seems to be answered after all, she suffers an agony which is, for her, a spiritual rebirth; after that, the journey to the 'wool mountains' is not necessary.

Catrin's experience might lead one to assume that her creator had no great opinion of organised religion, but Goronwy too has his encounter with the Establishment in the shape of the Pontargele curate, Ivor Owen, and he makes an interesting comparison between the showy new church with its social climber congregation and the old mountain church where all is simple and decent, and the country people come. Allen Raine evidently rejected the Nonconformist tradition in favour of the Anglican form of worship, but she retained many of the attitudes of Nonconformity.

Although A WELSH WITCH cannot be regarded as a complete success, it was undoubtedly its author's most ambitious book, in length as well as range, and after it she seems to have been temporarily exhausted. (Its writing, of course, went on during the early period of Beynon Puddicombe's illness, and this in itself must have imposed a considerable strain.) She continued to write—the annual book was an estab-

48

lished tradition—but neither ON THE WINGS OF
THE WIND nor HEARTS OF WALES, her next two
books, can be regarded as up to the standard of
A WELSH WITCH. Both are set in or near Newcastle
Emlyn, which appears in one as 'Tregarreg' and
in the other in a medieval disguise, and they
show the results of both her childhood study of
the local 'characters' and her prolonged reading
of Sir Walter Scott's novels.

ON THE WINGS OF THE WIND is the tale of a family
feud. In years long past Matti Lloyd ran off,
accidentally, with Silvan Vaughan, and so sent
her sister Gwen into a state of quiet insanity
and ended her own engagement to 'Doctor Dan'.
Now, after Matti's death, her young niece Miriel
comes to know both Doctor Dan and Silvan
Vaughan's family; she is courted by Vaughan's
son, Iago, but eventually marries the doctor.
Meanwhile Silvan Vaughan himself brings Gwen
from her madness; both die reconciled and are
buried near Matti, while Silvan's niece and h·s
elder son, Phil, repeat (with a happy ending) the
story of Matti and Silvan. There is the usual
careful, loving description of the setting and the
characters who fill it, especially Peggi Doll and
her husband, who were apparently real people,
but seem almost too Dickensian to be true, and
the two sets of servants, Betti and Deio at Tregarreg, and Stivin Storrom and Mali at Doloer,
Miriel's home. But though the novel is very
readable, there is something tired, almost flat
about it, as though its author no longer had the
energy to build to climaxes, or give the necessary
light and shade.

Interestingly, there is one passage which, though part of a conversation on a windy night, is in fact a very effective short story, and one which has a certain kinship with the work of Caradoc Evans. It is the macabre tale of a man so mean that, after more or less starving his wife to death, he steals her wedding ring from the coffin to use if he marries again. When she wished, Allen Raine could be as cutting in a few short phrases as Caradoc Evans could in a whole story; she had as few illusions about her neighbours, but rather more charity. (Incidentally, ON THE WINGS OF THE WIND contains Allen Raine's only portrait of a 'bard', but the farmer Iago, with his *youthful figure and pale intellectual face* is a very long way from the wild-eyed poetic seers of other romancers; he has more in common with Dic Jones than Dylan Thomas.)

HEARTS OF WALES is Allen Raine's only attempt at a completely historical novel, and though it is pleasant enough, it cannot be said to be a great success as a portrait of the period of Owain Glyndŵr. It describes the adventures of Eleri of Garth, whose father, on his deathbed, commits her to the care of his brother Gwythern. Gwythern is a rogue, whose gloomy castle of Twr-y-Graig, set in a forest near Newcastle Emlyn, is a robbers' nest, and he plans to replace Eleri with his own daughter Indeg, and so capture Newcastle Emlyn from its dying lord (another brother). His plot fails, and Eleri is rescued by Deraint ap Rhys, the new lord of Emlyn. There is also a sub-plot involving Deraint and his two childhood friends, Seithyn Owen (alias Derinos, the traitor) and Iestyn Mai who has become a 'sin-eater'. The working title for the novel was actually THE SIN EATER and possibly the sub-plot, with its study of human ties and weaknesses, was of more concern to Allen Raine than the adventures of the somewhat passive Eleri, who is not one of her more interesting heroines. According to her diary THE SIN EATER was begun in January 1903, and she was working on the third chapter by 13th January, when she says *Put aside Sin eater for the present having found out that the true history of Emlyn Castle does not tally with it.* However by 25th January she had recommenced work on it, and from then on proceeded briskly, writing as many as nine pages in a session.

As a historical novel, HEARTS OF WALES leaves much to be desired. Its official setting is the period of the Glyndŵr rebellion, but this comes into the story only twice, and then indirectly. Instead of political or social history, we have a kind of medieval extravaganza typified by the treatment of the sin-eater (whose job is literally to eat a dead man's sins, as symbolised by food left in a dish on top of the corpse). There are a few very faint echoes of Sir Walter Scott, but the novel has far more kinship with the tradition of the Gothic romance, being strong on atmosphere but decidedly weak on action. Iestyn Mai, the sin-eater, is a somewhat ironic figure; he is a Lollard, does not believe in the saints or religious ritual, and only pretends to eat the symbolic meal—not through any superstitious fears, but to avoid the possibility of infection. In a sense Allen Raine too is both having her cake and eating it here; she uses the picturesque but barbarous custom, but in such a way as to excuse her compatriots for having believed in it.

Both ON THE WINGS OF THE WIND and HEARTS OF WALES sold well, as usual, and though artistically they are less ambitious than the earlier novels, they had their own importance in their author's development. As has been suggested, A WELSH WITCH marks the end of one line of growth, and perhaps a beginning of something new, and the two books that followed were to some extent trial runs for future work. The plot became less important, and instead the emphasis was placed on the relationship of the characters themselves and their inner life. Furthermore, though the books were still basically romances, there was no longer the same insistence on a happy ending for everyone. The hero and heroine had still to be united, of course, but even that union was no longer quite so inevitable, and the supporting characters did not automatically wander off into a neat disposal. In ON THE WINGS OF THE WIND Iago goes home to his empty farm and his poetry; though Silvan Vaughan dies peacefully and is buried beside Matti and Gwen, one is aware of the waste of the three lives rather than of any ultimate happiness beyond death. (One can compare this with TORN SAILS, where the deaths of Hugh Morgan and Mari Vone lead to a union impossible in life.) The same is true of HEARTS OF WALES where neither Iestyn Mai nor Derinos survive. Allen Raine did not revert to the kind of social novel that she had attempted in GARTHOWEN; instead she accepted the romantic element and created her story out of the emotional entanglements of the characters and the resulting conflicts.

Although only two of her first seven books were strictly historical—WHERE BILLOWS ROLL was set circa 1840—all of them were to some extent uncontemporary. Their author was in her sixties, and, in the beginning at least, was writing about a society in which she had not been living for over twenty years, and it was thus inevitable that though she was aware of the overall pattern of life there, she was not concerned with the burning issues of the day. This gives a timeless quality to the writing, and though one can turn to the sociologist for confirmation of the accuracy of the way of life depicted, there is no real gap of years between the picture of Ynysoer in 1840 in WHERE BILLOWS ROLL and the same place in (presumably) 1899 in BY BERWEN BANKS. However after 1900 Allen Raine was once more part of her community—and not the secluded invalid that some later reports suggested. Perhaps this was one reason for taking Newcastle Emlyn as the setting for ON THE WINGS OF THE WIND and HEARTS OF WALES; she could write of a remembered Tresaith at a distance, but when she was once more part of the reality she needed time to assimilate the changes that had taken place since the long summers at Glandwr in the eighteen fifties and sixties. This she had done by the time that she came to write QUEEN OF THE RUSHES, for all practical purposes her last book.

Whatever the strict orthodoxy of her religious beliefs, Allen Raine was much concerned with spiritual matters, and it was only to be expected that she would be interested in the religious revival that was taking place in West Wales at the time. The 1904 Revival began in the area round Newcastle Emlyn, and so she had every opportunity to study the movement, which differed from the Methodist Revival of the eighteenth century in that it was a very 'willed' affair, with little or no intellectual basis. It is clear from the writings, autobiographical and otherwise, of the men involved in the 1904 Revival that they were not merely waiting and hoping for spiritual regeneration, they were actively prodding the Holy Spirit into a manifestation. There was at the time a reaction against materialism and against 'social' churchgoing, and a movement towards greater personal holiness, but this was not enough for men like Seth Joshua and Evan Roberts. This atmosphere of spiritual ferment was the setting for what may be described as the first meetings of the Revival at New Quay and Newcastle Emlyn in September, 1904.

Evidently Allen Raine was much concerned with the movement from its earliest days, and on 31st December, 1904, at a time when there was little or no public questioning of the Revival, the WESTERN MAIL published a letter by her.

I approach the subject of the revival in Wales with great hesitation, so unsatisfactory to me are its present manifestations, so vast are its possibilities for the future of the nation. I venture to hope, nay, to believe, that the awakening and upheaval in spiritual life which we see around us, is caused by a real influx of the Spirit of God; and if that be the case, how great a responsibility rests upon the leaders of the movement, more especially upon the ministers of religion.

The sensitiveness to religious feelings, the enthusiasm, the warmth of the Cymric nature, are particularly adapted to a grand reformation, to which I believe, this present revival may be but the preparation and precursor. The Welsh word 'diwygiad' expresses better what we want in Wales than the English word 'revival', for it implies reform as well as repentance.

I am far from denying that a sudden conversion is possible —we have many examples of it in the history of religion— but I think it is rare, and that a sudden conviction of sin is very frequently mistaken for 'conversion' in the present revival; hence the scenes of frenzied excitement which are calculated to bring ridicule upon a movement which, if guided into the proper channels, might be for the uplifting of the nation.

Public-houses deserted, happiness and love restored to ruined homes are glorious tributes to the force of the revival, to its undercurrent of spiritual strength. How great, therefore, will be our responsibility, more especially that of the ministers of religion, if this great spiritual awakening is allowed to pass away from our land without being followed by a real reformation in our national character.

Let the leaders of this great movement, therefore, impress upon their converts what a true diwygiad means. There are many traits in the Welsh character of which we are justly proud; there are, also, many faults, of which we are bitterly ashamed. Let the full force of this Pentecostal wave be turned upon our national sins, let us become a truthful, a sober nation; let us lead cleaner and purer lives; then, indeed, the revival will have proved to be a blessed uplifter to our land.

It is evident from this that she was particularly worried lest the extravagances of behaviour which accompanied many of the revival meetings

should both bring a much-needed spiritual reformation into disrepute, and also prove an
extremely shaky foundation for any permanent
improvement in the religious and moral life of
Wales. This was not an attitude likely to appeal
to the evangelists or their congregations, but it
formed the basis for QUEEN OF THE RUSHES which
appeared in May, 1906, the same month in
which Beynon Puddicombe died.

QUEEN OF THE RUSHES is set once more on the
Cardiganshire coast. Gwenifer Owen and Gildas
Rees are orphaned when their parents are
drowned, and Gildas, despite his youth, takes
charge of Scethryg Farm and of the child
Gwenifer; eight years later he marries Nance
Ellis, another Scethryg 'pensioner'. Gwenifer has
come to love Gildas, but her dumbness (due to
the shock of seeing her mother drowned) sets
her apart in the community, until Captain Jack
comes to Tregildas village, sees her, and wants
to marry her. Meanwhile Nance, though she
marries Gildas, has been smitten, in a fairly
light-hearted fashion, with Captain Jack's charms.
Here, then, is what might be called the classic
Allen Raine quartet: A loves B who is married
to C who likes D—who loves A; but this time
it is not the romantic complications that set the
plot in motion.

Instead the Revival breaks out, and it is the effect
of this on the various characters, both lovers and
villagers, which causes the real damage. Nance,
because she lacks solidity, is inclined to extremes,
first in housekeeping where *as the months went by*

and she seemed every day to grow more shrewd, more sharp and overbearing, and to rule her household more vigorously, Gildas began to look grave sometimes, and then in her devotion to Brynzion Chapel: *Two or three times in the week the hearth at Scethryg was bare and empty in the evenings . . . for Nance was at the prayer meetings . . . and she grew more and more wedded to the services of the chapel.* Gwenifer, too, goes regularly to the meetings, but having more depth of character, is moved but not carried away, very much like Captain Jack who goes first in a sight-seeing mood, and then becomes a fairly regular visitor.

It is Gildas, however, whose attitude clearly represents that of Allen Raine herself. He is intensely reserved, a man who finds it hard to give voice to his feelings, and who is shocked at the lack of control displayed by the revivalists; finally Nance publicly prays for his conversion, and he happens to arrive at Brynzion in time to hear her, an event which is, practically speaking, the end of their marriage. And yet even Gildas does not deny the good that is also part of the Revival.

Brynzion had been for a whole year alternately buoyed up with hope and sunk in despair by the absence of the religious fervour which in other places had attended the revival services. True, Ebben Lloyd the carpenter had 'taken the pledge', and kept to it, thus changing the miseries of a drunkard's home into an earthly Paradise. True also, Jerri the boatman had become a sober man and a shining light in the congregation. The Sunday-school was well attended by pupils whose ages ranged from eighty years downwards. The quarrels and bickerings of the little village had disappeared —in fact, Tregildas had become a pattern village in its great

*desire for the coming of the Holy Spirit; but all this did
not satisfy Brynzion, for there had been none of the excitement
and uplifting that had marked the meetings of the other
chapels in the neighbourhood.*

Tregildas has already seen the fruits of its reformation, but the villagers are not content,
they must have the sound and fury too, and
when these do not occur they begin to look for
a scapegoat; Gildas is the obvious choice and
(with considerable help from Nelli Amos, care-
taker of Brynzion and a gossip with an ancient
grudge against Gildas's family), the villagers
begin to ostracise him. This boycott culminates
in the ultimate social sanction:

*Ierri was one of the reapers, having dared to defy the ill-will
of his neighbours . . . the strong, almost sacred, claims of
the harvest had appealed to him as it had to the rest of the
villagers, though with them the distrust and suspicion with
which they looked upon Gildas had outweighed every other
consideration. They risked the danger of being turned out of
their homes rather than help the man who had wilfully
opposed and rejected the sacred claims of the revival.*

Ironically, as Jerri points out to Nelli Amos, their
Deity is less bigoted; Gildas's barley and wheat
are exceptionally fine crops: '*If the Lord is willing
to give him such a harvest, surely we can help to gather it in?*'

Meanwhile Nance, too shallow a character to
control the feelings which the Revival has roused
in her, has allowed her old flirtation with Captain
Jack to grow into a guilty infatuation which turns
her even further against Gildas. The captain
himself has not encouraged her, and is attempting

58

to court Gwenifer, but Nance rows out to his
boat at night, after quarrelling with Gildas on
the beach, and then becomes half-crazed when
the captain rejects her. She runs away, and when
a corpse is washed up on the shore, the villagers
immediately assume that it is Nance, that Gildas
murdered her, and that he will be hanged.
However Gwenifer, whose speech has returned
as a result of shock at Nance's actions, clears
Gildas, and slowly the community returns to
normal. There is a fire at Scethryg and Nelli
Amos is blamed and cast out of Brynzion until
Gildas pleads for her readmittance. Then Nance
reappears, delirious from hunger and exposure;
Gildas takes her in, but she dies and after a while
Gildas and Gwenifer marry, leaving only Captain
Jack (whose role is very like that of Iago in ON
THE WINGS OF THE WIND) alone.

Once again the novel is a love story, but here
at last the action flows from the characters
themselves and not from any device in the plot,
since the Revival does not *cause* events, it merely
enhances tendencies already present, brings out
the bigotry and narrow-mindedness of the
village community, and in some provokes emotions too strong to be contained. As in almost all
the other novels, there is a richness of character
and setting quite apart from the main pro-
tagonists, and the community itself is a character,
with its sanctions and traditions exercised by the
villagers as a body. (Interestingly, considering
her background, Allen Raine rarely, if ever,
writes of her peasant characters as either a
Hardyesque 'chorus' or a gallery of quaint
rustics; they are distinct and recognisable people,

and people with whom she and her heroes and heroines identify.)

As a critical account of the Revival the novel has a validity and a tactfulness which are remarkable considering that it was written during the events which it describes. Allen Raine accepted much of the evangelical approach as is clear from the WESTERN MAIL letter, but she saw also that it had its problems and perversions, and the story of Nance's overheated emotions, and of the bigotry let loose among the villagers, demonstrates these in action in both the individual and the community. On the other hand she also illustrates the beneficial aspects of the Revival, as in the portrait of Ben, one of Gildas's farm servants; and it is Ben who publicly defends Gildas against Nelli Amos's malice:

'I tell thee, if every man was as upright as mishteer, there would be no need of being converted, and if thou hadst been truly converted thou wouldst know better what a good man is.'

It is evident that ethics played a large part in Allen Raine's own religious beliefs, a greater part perhaps than any ritual aspect; no doubt this was chiefly due to the Unitarian influences that had been so strong in her youth, but she lays much stress (though not too obviously) on the natural balance of events. For instance, Catrin, in A WELSH WITCH, is presented as one in the closest communion with God and nature; and yet we are also carefully shown that natural religion is not enough. Catrin prays for Yshbel's death, and though she repents almost at once, she must still endure the punishment of seeing Yshbel in mortal danger before she is forgiven and allowed to save her victim. This supernatural fitness of things has its equivalent in the natural sphere, where like goes with like, and it is a theme which runs through QUEEN OF THE RUSHES. Gildas and Gwenifer come from the same stock and the same place, and so make a pair. Nance and Captain Jack, on the other hand, though both Welsh, are 'mongrels' in that both represent a marriage between the peasant and the gentleman, and as such they must always be outsiders. It is almost an echo of Hardy's theme in JUDE THE OBSCURE, and it is an intellectual rather than a social unfitness. Hezekiah Morgan, Nance's grandfather, was a schoolmaster who married *a beautiful but uneducated peasant girl* whom he could not raise to *his own standards of grace and refinement,* and from then on his career slipped away from him. Nance herself clearly draws her shallowness and levity from her pretensions to gentility. Captain Jack is the opposite, a gentleman's son who ran wild as a lad and wasted his inheritance; now he lives almost a double life, speaking and behaving like his own crew, and yet also quite capable of taking *his place as a man of gentlemanly behaviour and educated speech and manners* when required. It is just this which causes the damage, when he passes the time of day in an elegant but meaningless flirtation with Nance; she takes him seriously.

Hutchinson were to publish four more books by Allen Raine, but QUEEN OF THE RUSHES was her last serious work. NEITHER STOREHOUSE NOR BARN, which appeared in 1908, just before her death, is something of a puzzle. In the fragmentary diary for 1903–1908, she comments on 18th January, 1903, *Began* NEITHER STOREHOUSE NOR BARN, but at this point she was also working on HEARTS OF WALES and it seems unlikely that she was writing two completely new novels at the same time during early 1903. If one was judging from internal evidence—style, themes, settings and so on—one would assume that NEITHER STOREHOUSE NOR BARN was a very early work, coming perhaps immediately after YNYSOER, and possibly the historical complications of HEARTS OF WALES caused Allen Raine to turn to a much earlier manuscript and to revise it for publication in case she was unable to complete her current book. Certainly, though the work proceeded rapidly the book did not appear for five years, and then only when its author was probably too ill to have produced anything else. It is something of a fairy tale, the story of a vicar's daughter who goes tramping through West Wales with a musical lad of gentry stock and so loses her reputation. They are, of course, happily reunited, both with each other and with the boy's long-lost uncle, after episodes of misery in Manchester and Liverpool, and settle down to life-long bliss in a woodland glade on the banks of a river not too far removed from the Teifi. The book is, like all its author's work, very readable, and has one or two interesting character studies, particularly Kitty Price, the villainess, and Mrs. Peris-Jones, the heroine's Manchester aunt. But generally speaking, it is a long way below the standard of novels like A WELSH WITCH or QUEEN OF THE RUSHES, often clumsily written and plotted, with its sentimentality

62

redeemed only by occasional snatches of ironic observation.

By 1908 Allen Raine had eight published novels to her credit, no mean achievement considering that her first novel had not appeared until 1897 (if one excepts the newspaper serialisation of YNYSOER). It becomes even more remarkable when one considers the circumstances of her life in the years between 1897 and 1908, when she was coping with a change of home, a husband who was mentally deranged and possibly violent, and her own fatal illness. For part of the time, certainly, Beynon Puddicombe was away in Dr. Griffiths's asylum in North Wales, but on 17th August, 1903, the diary comments *Heard from Miss Griffiths saying they would not be able to take dear Beynon back* (he was then at Bronmôr) and on the 19th, two days later, she confesses *Went up to Glandwr in the afternoon dear Beynon very bad I cried in coming home.* Beynon's presence in the house meant more work and less time for writing; it also seems to have imposed some extra social obligations, and even his monthly pension was often not paid until his wife had written to ask for it. He died on 29th May, 1906. Meanwhile Allen Raine more or less adopted her brother John's son Lyn, relying on him for support now that Beynon was presumably incapable. Lyn himself was evidently fond of the social round, and on the surface at least does not strike one as the kind of character whom his aunt would find entirely sympathetic; in 1903 he went to South Africa to make his fortune, coming home again briefly in May 1906, when he married. By July he and his

wife Jenny were sailing from Liverpool on their
way to Pretoria.

All this time Allen Raine was leading a comparatively energetic life, with visits to Manchester,
Liverpool, Clifton, London (usually on business—
she was having various contractual and financial
problems with her publishers who, she felt, were
underpaying her—or to such events as the
Women Writers' Dinner, though she was not
fond of this kind of party) and Llandrindod
Wells; she did much family visiting, went for
long walks around Tresaith, and did a certain
amount of housework. The cancer from which
she died confined her to bed at the last, but only
a year before, at the respectable age of seventy,
she had taken part in a special family performance
of her own dramatisation of A WELSH SINGER in
the Court House, Newcastle Emlyn. The performance was in fact a device to gain copyright
protection for the play, and since it was held at
2 p.m. on a Tuesday afternoon and seats were
priced at one guinea and five shillings respectively,
it is unlikely that it was a truly public occasion,
but Allen Raine is listed as playing both Shan
(the hero's foster-mother) and Catrin Howells
(mine hostess of the local inn). Certain of the
biographical accounts of these years tend to
suggest that she was rather more of an invalid
than was the case, and they picture her lying on
a sofa dictating her novels to her various nieces
and cousins, particularly Katie Jones. In fact she
does at times seem to have had some sort of
difficulty in writing and employed an amanuensis
for her novels, but even then she was able to
keep up her diary herself, though in something

64

of a scrawl. Naturally she received a number of letters from readers of her novels, including her fellow novelists Owen Rhoscomyl and Guy Thorne, as well as Father Ignatius of Llanthony who wrote to her asking if the setting of her novels was genuine, and if so, where he could find such an idyllic village. She wrote back to Father Ignatius who replied in his turn praising the healthiness and naturalness of her books and the religious flavour in them—but he noted with regret the omission of the name of Jesus; in due course Allen Raine assured him that her reverence for Christ was no less than his, though their points of view differed. It was a strange correspondence between the Unitarian and the Anglo-Catholic. Other, closer links were with the distinguished local antiquarians George Eyre Evans and Mr. and Mrs. Tobit Evans with whom she was on friendly visiting terms.

Although her husband's death was a very great sorrow, there must also have been an accompanying sense of relief; mental illness, by its nature, is as hard (or harder) for family or friends to bear as it is for the patient. Unhappily Allen Raine herself had only two more years to live, and though she had always the love and support of her brother and his family to help her, they could not prevent the pain of her illness. In this too she was part of her own community. She did visit London to consult a doctor there, but she also followed the country practice and consulted a herbalist in Gwbert who claimed to be able to cure cancer of the breast; his treatment did her no good, and may have done harm, but it was very much in the tradition of her native countryside that she should turn to the local *dyn hysbys* (wise man) in this way. A neighbour died of cancer shortly before her own death, and she commented '*Poor Sarah T— and I will be entitled to a long rest before we wake to our new life*', but her own last words, according to Elfed, were the simple promise of Job: *Though He slay me, yet will I trust in Him*. The doctor who attended her was Dr. Powell of Newcastle Emlyn — almost certainly Caradoc Evans's 'wicked uncle'.

When she died, she left behind the early unpublished novel YNYSOER, and an unfinished novel, UNDER THE THATCH, which she had begun on the evening of 5th November, 1906, the day before Beynon's former attendant, Ferrier, got married (an event which she underlined in her diary). Hutchinson, bereft of their best-selling author, tried to reap whatever harvest they could from these remnants, and duly published YNYSOER as WHERE BILLOWS ROLL in 1909; in 1908 they had published Allen Raine's collected short stories under the title of ALL IN A MONTH. As for UNDER THE THATCH, there was a suggestion that Owen Rhoscomyl, best known for his historical novels, should finish it; he was not unwilling, but said (21st July, 1908) that he would need to study the rest of her books, and the village of Tresaith, in order to get into the right frame of mind for the unfinished manuscript. He had a great admiration for Allen Raine, but either he finally decided that the work was beyond his capabilities or else the author's family objected, because eventually the book was completed by Lyn Evans (though with no official acknowledgement of the fact). This left UNDER THE THATCH as a rather strange mixture; even when one does not know that it is not entirely Allen Raine's work, the contradictions, both internal and with the attitudes and beliefs expressed in the earlier books, suggest that something very odd has occurred.

The original theme was apparently mercy-killing, said (in the publisher's list, not in the novel) to have been based on an actual event which came to the notice of the author, but this has been interwoven somewhat clumsily with an attack on quack doctors and a romance complicated by social inequalities. The three main characters are Barbara Owen, daughter of a gentry family that has fallen on hard times; Michael Lloyd, the miller's son who has become a distinguished doctor; and Essylt Lewis, a peasant girl of bad character and parentage, whom Michael once promised to marry. As the result of an accident Barbara's mother suffers from attacks of agonising pain which will eventually kill her. Michael gives Barbara medicine to relieve the pain, with a strict warning about the results of exceeding the prescribed amount, but Barbara, unable to stand the strain, gives her mother an overdose and Mrs. Owen dies. Essylt has seen this, and threatens Barbara; but the girl has troubles of her own, since she has cancer for which she is being treated by Rhysin Pengraig. Eventually Barbara is discovered not to have killed her mother, Essylt dies, and the way is clear for Barbara and Michael to marry.

Exactly how much of this Allen Raine wrote is unclear, but almost certainly the novel as published was not what she intended to write. The book was begun at the end of 1906, and we know that the first three chapters had been written by 30th November; at this point the author was still leading an active life, and if the novel remained unfinished, it seems probable that this was not solely due to illness. In fact, Barbara's position, once she has given the overdose, becomes quite untenable; she *has* killed her mother, however excellent the motive, and given Allen Raine's normal ethical approach, she must pay the penalty. The way out employed—of finding that the overdose was not the medicine but a harmless herbal extract meant for Essylt—is mere sophistry; for Allen Raine it was always the intention that counted.

Quite apart from this fudging of the moral issues, UNDER THE THATCH is also untypical of Allen Raine's work in its social references. Michael Lloyd is introduced as follows:

It would not have surprised her to see one of the usual type of Welsh peasant-student, that grasps so eagerly at the chance of learning, and makes such rapid strides in its pursuit, stunted in growth by hard work and privation endured in early youth . . . (But Michael Lloyd was) entirely free from the aggressive familiarity with which a man or woman of inferior education often attempts to bridge over the gulf which separates him from those more highly cultured than himself.

This is a very long way from Will Owen in GARTHOWEN. The same contradiction appears in several of the passages referring to Wales, which are very much 'tourist fodder', as for instance in a comment about the giver's polite concealment of the charitable intention of a gift: *Such a phrase is by no means unusual among the Welsh lower classes . . . 'charity' savoured of the 'House', and enforced life in that (although in comparison to the wretched cottages in which they usually lived, it was luxury) was deemed the greatest disgrace that could befall them.* This is not precisely uncomplimentary, but it is distanced from its subject in a way very unlike Allen Raine's normal attitude.

Mercy-killing is not as modern a subject as one might assume; in 1915 Ethel M. Dell used the same theme for her sequel to THE WAY OF AN EAGLE. But her heroine atones for her crime, whereas Barbara Owen remains self-righteous about the whole thing, and never really accepts the implications, moral or legal, of what she has done. In mid-flight, therefore, the book alters course slightly and concerns itself with Essylt and the evils of non-professional medicine. Essylt is not an attractive character; she is lazy, envious and spiteful, and even her physical appearance is repellent, a sort of garish beauty. Yet her comments and reactions are often true, even moral, and in some ways she is a more worthy figure than Barbara, while the nature of her illness and her suffering are such that the general condemnation of her seems, if not quite unjustified, certainly cruel in the extreme. This may well be due to Lyn Evans rather than to Allen Raine; possibly Essylt's role was originally quite different and the cancer theme was enlarged from an episode concerning a minor character to its present scope in order to allow

the co-author to express his anger at the quack-
doctor whom he believed to have harmed his
aunt. If so, it does Lyn Evans's heart rather more
credit than his literary sense. In any case, his
work on UNDER THE THATCH was clearly not just
a matter of completing the story; to judge from
the contradictions everywhere present, he re-
vised the entire manuscript according to his own
attitudes, so that one might well misquote the
old saying: It is interesting, but it is not Allen
Raine.

Most of Allen Raine's novels had been serialised,
in newspapers or magazines, and she had also
written a number of short stories of varying
length for magazine publication, but this was
not her medium. Of the eleven stories published
as ALL IN A MONTH, most are anecdotes or
sketches for novels, and only two or three
even approach the precision and completeness
demanded by the short story as a literary
form.

The title story, 'All in a Month', which had been
written before March, 1903, is probably of more
biographical than literary interest. It is set in a
'genteel Broadmoor', a private asylum in the
remotest part of North Wales, which is fairly
obviously based on Dr. Griffiths's establishment,
though the plot is an absurd complication of
murders, missing wills and unlikely coincidences.
But in her studies of insanity, here, in TORN SAILS,
and elsewhere, Allen Raine was surely trying to
come to terms with her husband's illness and
to reduce the problem to manageable
proportions.

70

Of the other stories, 'A Life's Chase', which won a place in the 1937 Faber collection of Welsh short stories, is effective, if not remarkable; 'Was It the Wind?', though flawed in its construction, is sufficiently eerie to raise a shiver in the reader, and 'A Step in the Dark!' is an enjoyable variation on the theme of the over-zealous deacon, almost good enough to be a folk tale. The nearest to a true short story, though, is perhaps 'Home, Sweet Home', a fairly late piece of work (from the autumn of 1906). It is the story of Nancy Vaughan of Bronwylan Farm, a widow whose son John sends her off to the Workhouse so that she will be no expense or trouble to his new wife. Nancy thinks she is going to live with her daughter, and is both horrified and ashamed when she learns where she is to be put, though, knowing her son's callousness, she is not dis-illusioned; her only prayer after that is that she shall not die in the Workhouse. Then, on Christ-mas Day, she finds a door open, and sets off for Bronwylan; it has been snowing and after a time she sits down to rest and falls asleep, dreaming that she is at home; her dead body is found the next day. The subject is one that gives every opportunity for sentimentality, but Allen Raine avoids the pitfalls with the skill of an expert. Nancy is well aware of her son's character, and once the initial shock has worn off, there is no attempt to pile on the horrors; the Workhouse matron is kindly, if businesslike, the food ad-equate, the other inmates friendly, if a trifle soured or odd. But Allen Raine understands the true misery of the place: *the large bare, room where some of the women were sewing, but most of them sitting with empty hands, and faces that grew daily more dull and hopeless*. Even the ending keeps its balance; the two men sent to look for Nancy *were delighted, for it meant a change in the monotony of their lives.*

Once one has grown used to the more expansive style, it is easy to forget that Allen Raine was writing almost a century ago; or that she was, in her own way, a pioneer in many of the subjects with which she deals, as in the unreverential tone of many of her references to religion. But in 'A Brave Welshwoman', the last story in ALL IN A MONTH, written within fifteen years of the now infamous Wounded Knee massacre, she describes her heroine's views on the Indian problem thus:

'Is it any wonder', Nellie would say, with her weak womanly arguments, 'that when we have stolen from them their lands and driven them from their wigwams, that they should be angry and vindictive? I believe that if they were kindly treated they would be less ferocious . . . I believe the 'whites' are every bit as cruel and vindictive to them as they are to us'.

In due course Nellie has the opportunity to test her theories when the homestead is surrounded by starving Indian braves. *In a minute Nellie understood, and the hospitable Welsh instinct awoke within her.* She feeds the Indians, who make no attempt to harm her or the house, and later, instead of the expected night attack, she is presented with a newly-killed deer as a thank-offering. (One realises the irony implicit in the earlier phrase *her weak womanly arguments.*) There cannot have been many in those days who would have put the Indian case so forcibly—and Allen Raine's books sold as widely in America as in Britain.

72

Regrettably, since her short stories are, on the whole, the least interesting part of her work, it is these stories which have brought her most of what little critical notice she has received in recent years, and, not surprisingly, most of that notice has been either hostile or dismissive. Gwyn Jones speaks of *the sentimental dynasties of Allen Raine and the Maid of Cefn Ydfa,* and Glyn Jones says (in THE DRAGON HAS TWO TONGUES) *inspired or not, (her stories) are not inspiring. Or rather, what they inspire is perhaps the line of whimsey and unreality we see as elements in the novels of Edith Nepean, Michael Gareth Llewellyn and Alexander Cordell, and which has its apotheosis in that staggering and accomplished piece of literary hokum* HOW GREEN WAS MY VALLEY.

While she was alive, Allen Raine enjoyed very good relations with the critics, both in London and in Wales where she was hailed above all for the authenticity of her writing; one Welsh critic, reviewing HEARTS OF WALES, commented: *Allen Raine has from her cradle been used to looking at Welsh life, not with borrowed, but with her own eyes, and it is this that, as a writer of Welsh fiction in English dress, gives her such advantage over those who only know the country and its folk from tourists' descriptions or the experience gleaned during a brief holiday.* (It is interesting to contrast this with D. Tecwyn Lloyd's comment in a recent PLANET article that *Allen Raine (Mrs. Puddicombe Beynon—sic) was a descendant of the well known Welsh divine and poet Dafydd Dafis, Castellhywel, but her own upbringing and most of her adult life had been English. She either had no direct knowledge of Welsh life or she has overlaid it in her novels with such a thick layer of romantic mush that it hardly makes any difference.*) But the critics were not merely admiring bystanders. A comparison with Sir Walter Scott was frequent, even from critics who were unlikely to know of Allen Raine's admiration for him, but it was generally recognised that her own achievement was on a much smaller scale—*Scott and water* as one reviewer put it.

Practising writers like Owen Rhoscomyl and Arthur Mee (editor of the WESTERN MAIL) drew attention to another aspect of Allen Raine's work—her success in popularising Wales as an acceptable subject for novelists; and Mee, in a review of NEITHER STOREHOUSE NOR BARN, made a further point, as relevant today as it was in 1908. *England never appreciated her Northern neighbour until Scott wrote for her and for the world his immortal novels. Had he written them in Gaelic they would have been a sealed book to the Englishman till this day. Had Allen Raine written in Welsh her novels would no more have moved the Saxon than did RHYS LEWIS. Let the Welshman foster his native tongue; but to move the Saxon he must do it in English . . . her pages contain no false impressions of a people who (as we know) are so easily misunderstood.* One may question the need *to move the Saxon,* of course, and rightly so; but in view of the unfortunate economic and social side-effects of non-Welsh views of Wales drawn from the accounts of tourists or native eccentrics, it must be admitted that the point is still valid. It has been suggested earlier that one mark of the true Anglo-Welsh writer is the ability and/or desire to act as a bridge between the various linguistic communities of Wales, and in these terms Allen Raine is quite certainly a 'founding mother'.

Inevitably her death presented something of a problem, not so much to the critics already described, but to those with literary pretensions, like Ernest Rhys. Their subject had written at length about Wales, and had been immensely successful; obviously she merited consideration —but then, she wrote romances, and romances were not Literature. In fact, Ernest Rhys's two appreciations, published in the MANCHESTER GUARDIAN on 24th and 27th June, 1908, are an odd mixture of genuine criticism and superficial summary. He had plainly read only some of Allen Raine's novels, but he took these as the norm, and remarks *While she wrote many novels, she only told one tale. It was in effect a Welsh love story, with a congenial group of people abetting or delaying its action but working to a happy close.* (Which is merely to state the recipe for a romance, whether it be PRIDE AND PREJUDICE or A VIRGIN IN PARIS). On the other hand he sees very clearly that Allen Raine was not strictly a contemporary writer: *(her) novels read like a survival of the day when novelists wrote from the heart and not from the nerves or from a critical conceit of life, as so many do today. Her method and her writing were old-fashioned, judged by theirs.* He comments that she was a product of the Eisteddfod, but then goes on to say of her characters: *She did not see them quite as they were; she made them pretty to look upon as a child would like to do. It is because of this pre-occupation of hers with one countryside seen through a kind of tinted glass that Welsh readers who wish to see Wales pictured as it really is were not satisfied to accept her as a genuine Welsh novelist.* This is one of the earliest examples of what were to become accepted critical truths; firstly that Allen Raine's view of life was purely sentimental and idealised, and secondly that her view of Wales and her own claim to Welshness were false. The first point has already been dealt with; as for the second, Ernest Rhys himself, as an expatriate, was perhaps not the best judge of 'Welshness', whatever that might be. O. M. Edwards, who was presumably at least as great an expert on the quality, specifically recommended A WELSH WITCH to his readers on the first page of the August 1907 copy of CYMRU'R PLANT along with novels by Owen Rhoscomyl, Daniel Owen and Winnie Parry.

A rather more informed commentator was Elfed, who paid an almost unwilling tribute to the novelist in the BRITISH WEEKLY on 25th June, 1908. *Her knowledge of the Welsh language was limited and uncertain; and the dialect she has used in her stories— never spoken of any human being—distressed those who knew Wales from within, and love its everyday speech. But even this thousands of Welsh readers largely forgave for the sake of the story.* (It should be remembered that Elfed had been a leading figure in the 1904 Revival, and as such he could hardly be expected to agree with the picture of Wales presented by the author of QUEEN OF THE RUSHES.) It is quite probable that after so many years in London, Allen Raine's Welsh was more than a little rusty, but the Evans family were Welsh-speaking—indeed, it is difficult to see how they could have managed in mid-nineteenth century Cardiganshire without a fluent grasp of their native tongue; the landed gentry, with imported servants, might not need Welsh, but the Evanses were in a rather different position. Elfed's opinion on the 'dialect' used in the novels is of particular interest as one of the first of many such criticisms levelled against Anglo-Welsh writers; Allen Raine could not reply, but later novelists, like Michael Gareth Llewellyn, insisted that the words their characters used were a true record of what they themselves had heard. (The question was, of course, complicated by the unfortunate influence of Caradoc Evans's pseudo-dialect on later writers.)

Allen Raine's knowledge of Welsh life and her attitude to Wales have already been discussed, and are amply illustrated in the novels. Her knowledge of Welsh culture is less obvious; in the novels there is one (incorrect) reference to the Mabinogion which the heroine of BY BERWEN BANKS is supposed to be reading to her uncle. (This, of course, is paralleled by the lack of reference to English literature.) But in 1897, the same year that saw the publication of A WELSH SINGER, she contributed a verse translation of Ceiriog's long poem 'Alun Mabon' to O. M. Edwards's magazine WALES. The translation is generally faithful to Ceiriog's work, but it is also effective as a poem, and indeed reads like an original with no evidence of the strain that can come from fitting the sense of one language into the sounds of another. As it happens, Allen Raine's version can be compared with another, slightly later translation by A. P. Graves (friend of Ceiriog and father of Robert Graves) who published his version in 1926. There is little to choose between the two for faithfulness to the sense of the original, though Allen Raine's version is more detailed, where Graves has a tendency to generalise; but when it comes to conveying the feeling of the poem, Allen Raine is definitely the more successful of the two, as can be seen from the following:

> *His birth was on the mountain side,*
> *And like the purple heather*
> *That grew beside his cottage door*
> *Through sun and stormy weather,*
> *He lived and grew, through sun and shade*
> *Upon the mountain side,*
> *And there, at last, like heather bloom,*
> *He withered and he died.*
>
> (A.R.)

> *Amid the mountains he was born*
> *And, like the flowerets glowing*
> *That gem the heath and gild the thorn,*
> *Our bonny boy kept growing.*
> *Within his veins he stored the sun,*
> *Withstood the wild hill weather,*
> *And when his earthly days were done,*
> *Passed like the purple heather.*
>
> (A.P.G.)

It is only in the last two stanzas, especially poignant today because of their sentiments about the continuance of the Welsh language, that Allen Raine is, for us, less moving than her successors.

Whatever the opinion of the critics, then or now, as to the merits of Allen Raine's work, her vast public had no doubts at all. Her sales were enormous, and THE BOOKMAN ranked her as one of the four best-selling novelists of the day (the other three were Marie Corelli, Hall Caine and Silas Hocking). Unfortunately her publisher's pre-war records were destroyed in the Blitz, so that figures of either sales or profits are almost impossible to gauge; but the eight books published before her death had sold just under two million copies between them in the United Kingdom and colonies by 1908; they were also published in America, and one was translated into French. Nor was her popularity a short-lived phenomenon; her novels were still being reprinted at least as late as 1930, and they appeared in several series of cheap editions, while in the early nineteen twenties TORN SAILS was made into a film by Leon M. Lion, a well-known London theatrical producer. Even when cheap editions of the novels appeared, they were relatively more expensive than today's paperbacks, and groups of friends would co-operate, each buying a different title so that they would have all the novels available in due course. And yet the author seems to have profited comparatively little from her success; when she died she left £8,573, ample, but no great fortune.

It is not usual for any prophet to be respected in his or her own country, and it is interesting to note that Allen Raine is even today remembered and admired in Tresaith; one man commented when her name was mentioned (Summer, 1977) that her books should be reprinted, they were much better than the *lwts* (filth) that comes out today. And yet she was by no means sparing of the less attractive characteristics of her neighbours; madness, meanness, cruelty, hypocrisy all appear in her pages and are condemned, if not explicitly, then effectively, as in the following speech from TORN SAILS.

'Oh, dir anwl!' said Sara spitefully, 'who could show pride to a poor humble creature like thee? I have seen how thou hast flattered and fawned upon her, but I don't think thy porridge will be any the thicker for it. As for me, I never cringe to anyone. My father was never suspected of sheep-stealing and my uncle's wife's brother never had occasion to keep accounts to satisfy his master. No! nor my mother never promised to make a quilt for four shillings and then charge six shillings for it!'

But she wrote from within, of 'our land', 'our national character' and never, as did many later novelists (for whatever reason) from the stand-point of an English audience.

As a novelist, Allen Raine is a somewhat ambiguous figure, not easily placed in any one category. She wrote romances and was a best-selling author, and yet there is more to her novels than can be covered by these headings; she wrote for and about Wales, and yet was read all over the world; her work was praised for its purity and sweetness, and yet can at times be as sharp as the most stringent critic could require. In fact there are three quite separate strands to all her work; first, the romantic plot; second, a celebration of the land and people of Wales; and third, a careful and lovingly observed study of Welsh society in nineteenth-century Cardigan-shire. It was her romantic plots, with their beautiful heroines, handsome heroes and im-probable vows which earned her the scorn of serious critics, though even these praised her ability to tell a tale; yet if one compares her characters and plots with those of other romantic novelists, then or now, one realises how much substance she was able to give to potentially cardboard creations. As for her celebration of Wales, that also, to modern tastes, is a little too flowery; the arrival of the film and television have done away with much of the need for detailed description. But here again the romantic haze is given substance by the author's precise knowledge of the scenes she describes:

A long, peaked headland stretched out on one side of the harbour, broken up at its farthest point into jagged rocks that rose out of the deep green waters at low tide, their surface covered with tufts of golden brown bladder-weed, under the clammy branches of which the crabs lived and throve. These rocks, with their myriad pools, were the favourite daily resort of the village children, who roamed there at low tide, springing from rock to rock, and hunting with never-failing interest in the fissures and crannies, sitting on their edges, with bare feet dangling in the sunny water, shouting to each other, and singing with boisterous, but musical, voices.

(From A WELSH WITCH)

It is, however, on the third component of her work that Allen Raine's reputation as a novelist must stand, on her picture of the society from which she came and in which she spent more than half her life. She was not a novelist of ideas, though there *are* ideas in her novels, and her achievement was therefore different in kind as well as in quality from that of, say, Thomas Hardy, a writer with whom she otherwise had much in common. But whatever the gap in accomplishment, it is writers like Hardy or Dickens or the Brontës whom Allen Raine's work calls to mind, and not the Victoria Holts or Georgette Heyers of her own day. Perhaps, had she started earlier or continued longer, she might eventually have developed into a novelist of equal standing with those already mentioned; it is impossible to say now, and all too easy to discover unfulfilled genius in writers who for one reason or another can be regarded as cut off in mid-career. One thing is clear, however, and that is that Allen Raine, like a number of other Anglo-Welsh writers (Jack Jones, for instance) tended to write below her own ability, to settle for the comparatively easy success of the fluent story-teller rather than to probe deeper into the underlying experience of the society portrayed.

As has been said earlier, it is the convention to assume that Anglo-Welsh prose effectively began with Caradoc Evans's MY PEOPLE, and that any real 'school' of Anglo-Welsh writers began in the Twenties and Thirties, when magazines like THE WELSH REVIEW and WALES provided a platform for a rich crop of young poets and short-story writers. This is true in so far as any self-conscious Anglo-Welsh grouping is concerned, and the writers of the Thirties and Forties (many of whom, of course, are still active today) certainly drew a great deal of impetus from Caradoc Evans, but it does not mean that there were no earlier writers, or that they never communicated with each other. In Allen Raine's case there is evidence that she corresponded with Owen Rhoscomyl (who, in his turn, influenced Roland Mathias towards an interest in Anglo-Welsh literature) and Guy Thorne, with George Eyre Evans, Tobit Evans and O. M. Edwards; whether she read the work of other Anglo-Welsh writers is not known, but she had certainly studied Welsh language writers like Ceiriog. Less easy to determine is the question of influence by Allen Raine on later writers, if it exists. Few, if any, of today's Anglo-Welsh writers have read her novels, which have been out of print since 1940; (though three have been translated into Welsh in recent years). However there are at least three directions in which her influence is in some degree apparent.

Firstly, there is the succession of romantic novels inaugurated by what Mrs. Hope of Llangrannog, an unofficial biographer, described as *a stupid, sentimental tale written by an Englishwoman without any knowledge of the country*—a fair comment on most of the same school. Allen Raine must be awarded much of the responsibility for these, not so much because of her own writing, as because of her success; for a time she made this sort of gush fashionable, but one suspects that both Allen Raine and Mrs. Hope would be as startled as they would be indignant to find critics placing her alongside these 'followers'.

Secondly, there is the direct and freely acknowledged influence of A WELSH SINGER on the playwright Emlyn Williams. It is an interesting story, because it also illustrates how comparatively unlikely it was for the average aspiring young Anglo-Welsh author of the 'First Flowering' to come into contact with Allen Raine's books

(Annie the maid) brought in something she had fished up from her tin trunk, a novel which had long ago frittered

away its cover. A WELSH SINGER *threatened religion, and I opened it gingerly . . . it was with a shock of pleasure that I turned the pages of my first real book. It was like hearing a vast wind, then looking up and seeing, beyond the Glanrafon woods, a curtain of cloud sweep up and away in gigantic folds, revealing the world . . . 'Allen Raine' had done this, a lady novelist who could have been dubbed the Marie Corelli of below stairs; but she wrote with sincerity and I am glad there was nobody to disillusion me.*

The third and last sphere of influence is more difficult to document, but it concerns Caradoc Evans, *the father of us all,* as Gwyn Jones calls him. Caradoc Evans and Allen Raine came from the same part of Wales; indeed Caradoc's uncle was in all probability the doctor attending Allen Raine at the time of her death, and Ada Puddicombe was an occasional visitor at Dyffryn Bern, the farm into which Caradoc's sister married. Caradoc Evans himself was nineteen when A WELSH SINGER appeared in 1897, and by then he was working in Cardiff as a draper's apprentice, but he can hardly have been unaware of his fellow-countrywoman's success, advertised nationwide as it was (sometimes luridly) by the various newspapers in which her novels were serialised. (In GIVE ME YESTERDAY James Williams, originally a native of Penbryn, comments on the local admiration for their 'own' best-selling author and the manner in which the novels were passed from hand to hand.) Both authors, the romancer and the satirist, thus shared a common subject matter; it is logical, therefore, to see certain resemblances and common themes, disguised though these may be by Caradoc Evans's style.

The story of Caradoc's discovery of the sources of this style—the Bible and Marie Lloyd—is well known, but the root of his decision to become a writer (and an English-language writer at that) is still apparently obscure. His early English stories show no sign of any remarkable control of the medium, and it must be admitted, as he did himself, that without those elements which caused such anger at home, his work might well have sunk without trace. Allen Raine's success, trumpeted everywhere, must surely have shown him both how he could make a living and (by using his neighbours as subject matter, just as she did) have his revenge on those who, he believed, had injured him. The style that he adopted was the equivalent of her story-telling ability, the sugar which attracted an audience to the serious content of the novels and short stories.

Ironically enough, when the furore over MY PEOPLE broke out in 1915, Caradoc's opponents used the name of Allen Raine as a rallying cry, opposing her *idyllic and charming* stories to the supposedly vile qualities of Caradoc's creations. The *leading solicitor* who was one of the earliest to write to the WESTERN MAIL was J. H. Evans, Allen Raine's brother John; he at least seems to have confined his criticism to the truth or otherwise of the picture of Wales shown in the book—and he may well have felt that he was in some sense defending his sister's memory. Otherwise the correspondence seems to have reflected little credit on either side, and naturally enough, after it Caradoc Evans was unlikely to have acknowledged even the slightest debt of kinship to Allen

Raine. And yet in the end the two writers were opposite sides of the same coin, and Gwen suffocating her dying baby with roast mouse in TORN SAILS is as much sister to Nanny in BE THIS HER MEMORIAL, as is the community drawn in TAFFY AT HOME, one of Caradoc's earliest published pieces, kin to the community that exists in all of Allen Raine's tales behind the romantic trappings, a world neither good nor bad, but simply human. It is her portrayal of this world that is Allen Raine's real achievement, one that retains its truth and vigour long after the romantic stories and the elaborate descriptions have become old-fashioned or obsolete.

A Select Bibliography

ALLEN RAINE

Novels
(Date of first British publication only)

A WELSH SINGER. Hutchinson, London, 1897.

TORN SAILS: A TALE OF A WELSH VILLAGE. Hutchinson, London: 1898.

BY BERWEN BANKS. Hutchinson, London, 1899.

GARTHOWEN: A STORY OF A WELSH HOMESTEAD. Hutchinson, London, 1900.

A WELSH WITCH: A ROMANCE OF ROUGH PLACES. Hutchinson, London, 1902.

ON THE WINGS OF THE WIND. Hutchinson, London, 1903.

HEARTS OF WALES: AN OLD ROMANCE. Hutchinson, London, 1905.

QUEEN OF THE RUSHES: A TALE OF THE WELSH REVIVAL. Hutchinson, London, 1906.

NEITHER STOREHOUSE NOR BARN. Hutchinson, London, 1908.

WHERE BILLOWS ROLL: A TALE OF THE
WELSH COAST. Hutchinson, London, 1909.
(As Ynysoer this won a first prize in the 1894
Caernarvon Eisteddfod; it was serialised at that
time in the NORTH WALES OBSERVER.)

UNDER THE THATCH. Hutchinson, London,
1910.

Short Stories

ALL IN A MONTH, AND OTHER STORIES.
Hutchinson, London. 1908.
(These stories had all appeared in magazine form,
sometimes in more than one place, during their
author's lifetime.)

Translations
By Allen Raine:

ALUN MABON. (Verse translation of Ceiriog's
poem). WALES, Vol. IV, 1897, pp. 3–4, 29–30, 78,
106–107, 127.

By Megan Morgan:

MYFANWY (A Welsh Singer), Cymdeithas Lyfrau
Ceredigion, Aberystwyth, 1960.

LLE TREIGLA'R DON. (Where Billows Roll).
Cymdeithas Lyfrau Ceredigion, Aberystwyth,
1964.

Calonnau Briw. (Torn Sails). Cymdeithas Lyfrau Ceredigion, Aberystwyth, 1968.

Miscellaneous

An Allen Raine Birthday Book. Hutchinson, London, 1909.

Biography and Criticism

There have been no full-length, or even substantial, accounts of Allen Raine or her work, and the main source for this essay, apart from the books themselves, has been the collection of material relating to Allen Raine recently deposited in the Carmarthen Record Office by her great-niece, Mrs. M. S. Beckingsale. The main printed sources quoted from in the text are listed below.

Mrs. K. Jones, Yr Ymofynydd, September, 1908, pp. 194–7.

Elfed, The British Weekly, 25th June, 1908.

Ernest Rhys, The Manchester Guardian, 24th and 27th June, 1908.

L. J. Roberts, The Welsh Review, Vol. I, No. 4, June, 1906, p. 94.

Emlyn Williams, George. Hamish Hamilton, London, 1961, pp. 47–52. Copyright © 1961 by Emlyn Williams.

James Williams, GIVE ME YESTERDAY. Gwasg Gomer, Llandysul, 1971, pp. 141–2.

Acknowledgements

I would like to express my thanks to all those who have helped me in the researching and writing of this essay. However I owe particular thanks to the following: West Glamorgan County Library and the Dyfed Archives Service for help in providing books and source material; the Rev. J. Towyn Jones for his advice and assistance; Mrs. Pamela Davies of Bangor for drawing my attention to the Emlyn Williams reference; Mrs. A. M. Jones of Carmarthen for information on Allen Raine's popularity in West Wales; and to Mr. A. B. Jones for encouragement, advice and assistance. Most of all, however, I would like to acknowledge both my debt and my gratitude to Mrs. M. Beckingsale of Newcastle Emlyn for her very generous hospitality and her assistance in my search for her great-aunt, Allen Raine.

The Author

Sally Jones was born in London in 1935, and educated at the University College of North Wales, Bangor, where she read History. She later worked as a reference librarian in Essex and Port Talbot. She has published articles on local history and on Anglo-Welsh writers and Anglo-Welsh children's books, as well as bibliographies on various subjects of Welsh interest, three books of verse, and a collection of children's stories. She is married, with three sons.

This Edition,
designed by Jeff Clements,
is set in Monotype Spectrum 12 Didot on 13 point
and printed on Basingwerk Parchment by
Qualitex Printing Limited, Cardiff

It is limited to 1000 copies of which this is

Copy No.   307

British Library Cataloguing in Publication Data

Jones, Sally
Allen Raine.—(Writers of Wales; ISSN 0141–5050).
1. Raine, Allen—Criticism and interpretation
I. Welsh Arts Council   II. Series
823′.8

ISBN 0–7083–0726–4